THE LITTLE BOOK OF HOURS

Praying with the Community of Jesus

REVISED EDITION

PARACLETE PRESS

Brewster, Massachusetts

The Little Book of Hours, Revised Edition

2007 First Printing Revised Edition

Copyright © 2003, 2007 by The Community of Jesus, Inc.

ISBN 13: 978-1-55725-533-4

Scripture quotations are from the *Holy Bible, New International Version*®. NIV®. Copyright © 1973, 1978, 1984 by International Bible Society. Used by permission of Zondervan Publishing House. All rights reserved.

The Library of Congress has catalogued the original edition as follows:
    The little book of hours : praying with the Community of Jesus.
        p. c.m.
        ISBN 1-55725-343-9
    1. Divine office—texts 2. Community of Jesus (Orleans, Mass.)
    BV199.D3L58 2003
    264'.15—dc21   2003013179

10 9 8 7 6 5 4 3 2 1

Published by Paraclete Press
Brewster, Massachusetts
www.paracletepress.com

Printed in China

CONTENTS

Introduction
vii

Prayer: Morning, Midday, and Vespers
Week 1
1

Week 2
61

Week 3
121

Week 4
181

Prayer: Compline
241

Prayers for Various Occasions
247

Notes
255

We gratefully acknowledge the Community of Jesus for granting us permission to use the several volumes of *The Liturgy of the Hours* as the basis of *The Little Book of Hours*. We also wish to thank Br. Benedict Young, cj, for the many hours he spent in compiling *The Little Book of Hours*.

INTRODUCTION

Y ou hold this *Little Book of Hours* in your hands because, like those of us who live here at the Community of Jesus, you believe that praying has something to do with living. It has a lot to do with living, as a matter of fact. In prayer we attend to the things about life that are of greatest importance to us—to the "one thing that is needful," as Jesus said to Martha—in other words, to the *One* whom we need above all others.

Prayer is first and foremost about relationship, our relationship with God and our relationship with one another in the Body of Christ. These relationships fill our lives with meaning and purpose. Prayer, then, is not so much an exercise of piety as it is an exchange of love.

The Community of Jesus is an ecumenical community in the Benedictine monastic tradition. As such, we come from diverse backgrounds and we represent a variety of vocations. Some of us are celibate sisters or brothers; some are married; some are single. Our homes are filled with young and old alike. But, within our diversity we find a single purpose—seeking to live our lives to the glory of God—and for this reason we have come together to live and to pray.

This is because we believe that the principal values espoused by monasticism through the centuries can be embraced in some way by every Christian. St Benedict may have written his "rule" for monastic living in the sixth century (by then there had already lived many generations of men and women monastics), but his exhortations still ring true in the twenty-first: Seek to love God above all else; listen intently to the Word of God so that it might direct and shape your life; find the presence of Christ in all whom you meet; weave together your work and prayer into a daily offering of praise to God. As we say in our own *Rule of Life for the Community of Jesus*:

> God's call is pure gift, and our grateful response, made possible by his grace, is the complete offering of our lives to him and to his service. . . . It is our joyful and solemn "yes" to this call that has brought us from our various backgrounds to form a united body of believers who seek to express a sacred vocation in the ordinary routines of daily life together.

In our community, we think of prayer as our common heartbeat, that rhythmic and unceasing exchange of receiving and giving that sustains our lives. "Pray without ceasing," wrote the apostle Paul (1 Thessalonians 5:17). But for prayer to happen at *all* times, it must happen at *some* time. As Karl Rahner, the great Catholic theologian, wrote: "I now see clearly that, if there is any path at all on which I can approach [God], it must lead through the middle of my ordinary daily life." And so, like countless monastic communities before us, we draw upon an ancient tradition of the church, sometimes called the Liturgy of the Hours, that punctuates the day with prayer at certain times: morning, noon, evening, and night.

Morning Prayer or *Lauds* (Latin for "praise") is the first prayer of the day, offering a new song of praise to the glory of God. *Midday* prayer speaks for itself. It is brief and concise, for it is offered in the midst of the busy day, reminding us that God alone is the one who gives meaning to our labors. *Evening Prayer* or *Vespers* (Latin for "evening star") is a prayer of thanksgiving as we look back on the day, giving thought to our own shortcomings and, above all, remembering God's ample blessings. Lastly, *Compline* (from the Latin for "complete" or "finished") closes the day, as we commend ourselves to God's care through the night.

At these four "hours" of each day—early in the morning, at noon-time, at the close of the work-day, before retiring—we make the brief walk to the Church of the Transfiguration, which stands at the center of our community, we vest in white alb and pectoral cross (symbols of our monastic vows), and we take our designated seat in choir. There we chant the psalms, listen to the readings, silently meditate upon what we have heard, and make our intercessions for the needs of others.

The Little Book of Hours is a shortened version of our community's prayer book, and all of its elements are drawn from the actual prayers that we make each day. A brief look at the table of contents will show you that Lauds, Midday, and Vespers are structured in a four-week cycle, while Compline remains the same every day (as the "bedtime" hour it might eventually be prayed from memory).

It may be helpful to consider each "hour" as a sacred dialogue with God which, like any dialogue, is made up of times to speak and times to listen. In the first segment, after gathering our thoughts and quieting our minds, we begin to speak. Through introductory sentences, an opening prayer, and a psalm, we address God. The second segment is a time to listen. It consists of a reading (though not at Midday—remember, this is just a quick stop in the day) and a space for reflection. This period of silence might be a good time to ponder certain questions: What word or phrase seems to "light up" from this reading? What does God seem to be saying *to me* through this word? What would I say to God in response? This leads to the final segment, when once again we speak, through closing prayers (the Appendix includes additional prayers for various needs and occasions), through the Lord's Prayer, and through asking God's blessing upon ourselves and our loved ones.

Finally, though the "Liturgy of the Hours" at the Community of Jesus is essentially communal, *The Little Book of Hours* has been designed so that it can be used either in small groups—certain lines have been italicized for use as responses—or in private prayer. In either case, whether alone or with others, consider saying these prayers aloud, so that you can both speak and listen to the words. (Once upon a time, all reading meant reading out loud, for this very reason.) Doing so may help to remind you that not only are you praying "with the Community of Jesus," but also you are actually taking part in a much larger and eternal conversation.

When we gather each day in our church we also hope to be reminded of this abiding truth. In our prayer we pay attention as the Holy Spirit breathes God's message of grace to us, and we breathe back our own words and songs of gratitude and praise. We call out to the heart of God, and we listen to the word of God as it has been given through the centuries—through the Scriptures, through psalms and canticles, through some of the church's great teachers and writers. When we pray, we add our own voices to this ceaseless chorus, taking our part in the song that has been sung since creation began. As one Orthodox theologian has put it, "You must never think that you pray alone, for even in your closet the host of heaven is with you." Prayer, whether made in private or in the company of others, is the way by which we join in earth's refrain to heaven's hymn.

WEEK 1

MORNING PRAYER

Sunday
Week 1

O Lord, open my lips.
And my mouth will proclaim your praise.

OPENING PRAYER

May our compassionate God drive away all our anguish, bestow health, and give us by the loving-kindness of the Father, the kingdom of the heavens. Amen.*

PSALM 95:1–7a

Come, let us sing for joy to the LORD; let us shout aloud to the Rock of our salvation. Let us come before him with thanksgiving and extol him with music and song.

For the LORD is the great God, the great King above all gods. In his hand are the depths of the earth, and the mountain peaks belong to him. The sea is his, for he made it, and his hands formed the dry land.

Come, let us bow down in worship, let us kneel before the LORD our Maker; for he is our God and we are the people of his pasture, the flock under his care.

READING
Thomas à Kempis
Write my words on your heart and meditate diligently on them, for in the time of temptation they will be very necessary for you. What you do not understand as you read, you will understand in the day of visitation.

SPACE FOR REFLECTION

BENEDICTUS
Canticle of Zechariah: Luke 1:68–79
"Praise be to the Lord, the God of Israel, because he has come and has redeemed his people. He has raised up a horn of salvation for us in the house of his servant David (as he said through his holy prophets of long ago) salvation from our enemies and from the hand of all who hate us—to show mercy to our fathers and to remember his holy covenant, the oath he swore to our father Abraham: to rescue us from the hand of our enemies, and to enable us to serve him without fear in holiness and righteousness before him all our days.

And you, my child, will be called a prophet of the Most High; for you will go on before the Lord to prepare the way for him, to give his people the knowledge of salvation through the forgiveness of their sins, because of the tender mercy of our God, by which the rising sun will come to us from heaven to shine on those living in darkness and in the shadow of death, to guide our feet into the path of peace."

CLOSING PRAYERS
Lord, have mercy.
Christ, have mercy.
Lord, have mercy.

Our Father, who art in heaven. . . .

Lord, hear my prayer.
And let my cry come unto you.

COLLECT
Almighty and ever-living God, we confidently call you Father as well as Lord. Renew your Spirit in us to make us more perfectly your children, that we may joyfully receive your promised inheritance. We ask this through our Lord Jesus Christ your Son, who lives and reigns with you and the Holy Spirit, one God forever and ever. Amen.

Lord, hear my prayer.
And let my cry come unto you.
Let us bless the Lord.
Thanks be to God.

May the souls of the faithful
by the mercy of God rest in peace.
Amen.
May divine help always be with us.
And with those who are absent from us.
Amen.

MIDDAY SERVICE

Sunday
Week 1

O God, come to my assistance.
O Lord, make haste to help me.

OPENING PRAYER

Mighty Ruler, true God, you who regulate the functions of all things and provide the morning its splendor, the midday its heat. Extinguish the flames of quarrels, take away harmful passions, grant healing of body and true peace of heart. Amen.

PSALM 1:1–3

Blessed is the man who does not walk in the counsel of the wicked or stand in the way of sinners or sit in the seat of mockers. But his delight is in the law of the LORD, and on his law he meditates day and night.

He is like a tree planted by streams of water, which yields its fruit in season and whose leaf does not wither. Whatever he does prospers.

SPACE FOR REFLECTION

CLOSING PRAYERS

Let your mercy, O Lord, be upon us.
As we have hoped in you.

Lord, have mercy.
Christ, have mercy.
Lord, have mercy.

Our Father, who art in heaven. . . .

Lord, hear my prayer.
And let my cry come unto you.
Let us bless the Lord.
Thanks be to God.
May divine help always be with us.
And with those who are absent from us.
Amen.

VESPERS

Sunday
Week 1

O God, come to my assistance.
O Lord, make haste to help me.

OPENING PRAYER
O Light, blessed Trinity and perfect Unity, already the fiery sun is receding; pour the light of your presence into our hearts. Amen.

PSALM 111
Praise the LORD. I will extol the LORD with all my heart in the council of the upright and in the assembly. Great are the works of the LORD; they are pondered by all who delight in them. Glorious and majestic are his deeds, and his righteousness endures forever.

He has caused his wonders to be remembered; the Lord is gracious and compassionate. He provides food for those who fear him; he remembers his covenant forever.

He has shown his people the power of his works, giving them the lands of other nations. The works of his hand are faithful and just; and all his precepts are trustworthy. They are steadfast for ever and ever, done in faithfulness and uprightness. He provided redemption for his people; He ordained his covenant forever—holy and awesome is his name. The fear of the LORD is the beginning of wisdom; all who follow his precepts have good understanding. To him belongs eternal praise.

GOSPEL READING
John 1:1–5

In the beginning was the Word, and the Word was with God, and the Word was God. He was with God in the beginning.

Through him all things were made; without him nothing was made that has been made. In him was life, and that life was the light of men. The light shines in the darkness, but the darkness has not understood it.

SPACE FOR REFLECTION

MAGNIFICAT
The Canticle of Mary: Luke 1:46b–55

"My soul glorifies the Lord and my spirit rejoices in God my Savior, for he has been mindful of the humble state of his servant. From now on all generations will call me blessed, for the Mighty One has done great things for me—holy is his name. His mercy extends to those who fear him, from generation to generation. He has performed mighty deeds with his arm; he has scattered those who are proud in their inmost thoughts. He has brought down rulers from their thrones but has lifted up the humble. He has filled the hungry with good things but has sent the rich away empty. He has helped his servant Israel, remembering to be merciful to Abraham and his descendants forever, even as he said to our fathers."

CLOSING PRAYERS
Lord, have mercy.
Christ, have mercy.
Lord, have mercy.

Our Father, who art in heaven. . . .

Lord, hear my prayer.
And let my cry come unto you.

COLLECT
Almighty and ever-living God, we confidently call you Father as well as Lord. Renew your Spirit in us to make us more perfectly your children, that we may joyfully receive your promised inheritance. We ask this through our Lord Jesus Christ your Son, who lives and reigns with you and the Holy Spirit, one God forever and ever. Amen.

Lord, hear my prayer.
And let my cry come unto you.
Let us bless the Lord.
Thanks be to God.

May the souls of the faithful
by the mercy of God rest in peace.
Amen.
May divine help always be with us.
And with those who are absent from us.
Amen.

MORNING PRAYER

Monday
Week 1

O Lord, open my lips.
And my mouth will proclaim your praise.

OPENING PRAYER
Lord Jesus, Splendor of the Father's glory, O true Sun, descend, sparkling with uninterrupted brightness; O radiance of the Holy Spirit, pour in upon our senses. Amen.

PSALM 24
The earth is the LORD'S, and everything in it, the world, and all who live in it; for he founded it upon the seas and established it upon the waters. Who may ascend the hill of the LORD? Who may stand in his holy place? He who has clean hands and a pure heart, who does not lift up his soul to an idol or swear by what is false.

He will receive blessing from the LORD and vindication from God his Savior. Such is the generation of those who seek him, who seek your face, O God of Jacob.

Lift up your heads, O you gates; be lifted up, you ancient doors, that the King of glory may come in. Who is this King of glory? The LORD strong and mighty, the LORD mighty in battle. Lift up your heads, O you gates; lift them up, you ancient doors, that the King of glory may come in.

Who is he, this King of glory? The LORD Almighty—he is the King of glory.

READING
Hal M. Helms

I the Lord am holy. I the Lord call you, my son, to greater holiness—holiness of thought, holiness of purpose. I am fashioning a people who bear the marks of my nature, who will be my witness in the present age, and will be with me in the ages to come.

SPACE FOR REFLECTION

CLOSING PRAYERS
Lord, have mercy.
Christ, have mercy.
Lord, have mercy.

Our Father, who art in heaven . . .

Lord, hear my prayer.
And let my cry come unto you.

COLLECT

Almighty and eternal Father, a new day
dawned when your only-begotten Son came
among us. Grant that we who share in his
human nature may also share in the kingdom
of his glory. We pray this through the same
Jesus Christ your Son, who lives and reigns
with you and the Holy Spirit, one God forever
and ever. Amen.

Lord, hear my prayer.
And let my cry come unto you.
Let us bless the Lord.
Thanks be to God.

May the souls of the faithful
by the mercy of God rest in peace.
Amen.
May divine help always be with us.
And with those who are absent from us.
Amen.

MIDDAY
SERVICE

Monday
Week 1

O God, come to my assistance.
O Lord, make haste to help me.

OPENING PRAYER

O Christ, you are the Light, the Splendor of the Father, and the eternal Hope of all things. Listen to the prayers which your servants throughout the world pour forth. Amen.

PSALM 13

How long, O LORD? Will you forget me forever? How long will you hide your face from me? How long must I wrestle with my thoughts and every day have sorrow in my heart? How long will my enemy triumph over me?

Look on me and answer, O LORD my God. Give light to my eyes, or I will sleep in death; my enemy will say, "I have overcome him," and my foes will rejoice when I fall.

But I trust in your unfailing love; my heart rejoices in your salvation. I will sing to the LORD, for he has been good to me.

SPACE FOR REFLECTION

CLOSING PRAYERS
Let your mercy, O Lord, be upon us.
As we have hoped in you.

Lord, have mercy.
Christ, have mercy.
Lord, have mercy.

Our Father, who art in heaven. . . .

Lord, hear my prayer.
And let my cry come unto you.
Let us bless the Lord.
Thanks be to God.
May divine help always be with us.
And with those who are absent from us.
Amen.

VESPERS

Monday
Week 1

O God, come to my assistance.
O Lord, make haste to help me.

OPENING PRAYER

Pour into us now, O most loving One, the gift of eternal grace, so that, by the misfortunes of new deception, old error may not destroy us. Amen.

PSALM 8

O LORD, our Lord, how majestic is your name in all the earth!

You have set your glory above the heavens. From the lips of children and infants you have ordained praise because of your enemies, to silence the foe and the avenger.

When I consider your heavens, the work of your fingers, the moon and the stars, which you have set in place, what is man that you are mindful of him, the son of man that you care for him? You made him a little lower than the heavenly beings and crowned him with glory and honor.

You made him ruler over the works of your hands; you put everything under his feet: all flocks and herds, and the beasts of the field, the birds of the air, and the fish of the sea, all that swim the paths of the seas.

O LORD, our Lord, how majestic is your name in all the earth!

GOSPEL READING
John 1:6–9

There came a man who was sent from God; his name was John. He came as a witness to testify concerning that light, so that through him all men might believe. He himself was not the light; he came only as a witness to the light. The true light that gives light to every man was coming into the world.

SPACE FOR REFLECTION

CLOSING PRAYERS
Lord, have mercy.
Christ, have mercy.
Lord, have mercy.

Our Father, who art in heaven. . . .

Lord, hear my prayer.
And let my cry come unto you.

COLLECT

Almighty and eternal Father, a new day dawned when your only-begotten Son came among us. Grant that we who share in his human nature may also share in the kingdom of his glory. We ask this through the same Jesus Christ your Son, who lives and reigns with you and the Holy Spirit, one God forever and ever. Amen.

Lord, hear my prayer.
And let my cry come unto you.
Let us bless the Lord.
Thanks be to God.

May the souls of the faithful
by the mercy of God rest in peace.
Amen.
May divine help always be with us.
And with those who are absent from us.
Amen.

MORNING PRAYER

Tuesday
Week 1

O Lord, open my lips.
And my mouth will proclaim your praise.

OPENING PRAYER

O Christ, dispel sleep, break the chains of night, release long-standing sin, and pour in new light. Amen.

PSALM 29

Ascribe to the LORD, O mighty ones, ascribe to the LORD glory and strength. Ascribe to the LORD the glory due his name; worship the LORD in the splendor of his holiness.

The voice of the LORD is over the waters; the God of glory thunders, the LORD thunders over the mighty waters. The voice of the LORD is powerful; the voice of the LORD is majestic. The voice of the LORD breaks the cedars; the LORD breaks in pieces the cedars of Lebanon. He makes Lebanon skip like a calf, Sirion like a young wild ox.

The voice of the LORD strikes with flashes of lightning. The voice of the LORD shakes the desert; the LORD shakes the Desert of Kadesh. The voice of the LORD twists the oaks and strips the forests bare. And in his temple all cry, "Glory!"

The LORD sits enthroned over the flood; the LORD is enthroned as King forever. The LORD gives strength to his people; the LORD blesses his people with peace.

READING
Robert Benson

There is another side to our prayer. It is the part of our life of prayer that recognizes that we are not really alone when we pray—the side of our prayer that links us to all who have gone before and who will come after us.

SPACE FOR REFLECTION

CLOSING PRAYERS
Lord, have mercy.
Christ, have mercy.
Lord, have mercy.

Our Father, who art in heaven. . . .

Lord, hear my prayer.
And let my cry come unto you.

COLLECT

O living and eternal God, you are more ready to give than we to ask. Grant us a new vision of yourself, that seeing you as you are, we may desire you, and desiring you, may surrender our lives to you. We ask this through our Lord Jesus Christ your Son, who lives and reigns with you and the Holy Spirit, One God forever and ever. Amen.

Lord, hear my prayer.
And let my cry come unto you.
Let us bless the Lord.
Thanks be to God.

May the souls of the faithful
by the mercy of God rest in peace.
Amen.
May divine help always be with us.
And with those who are absent from us.
Amen.

23

MIDDAY SERVICE

Tuesday
Week 1

O God, come to my assistance.
O Lord, make haste to help me.

OPENING PRAYER

O Jesus, our redemption, love, and desire, may your love constrain you to pass over our evils, sparing us, and having answered our prayer, may you satisfy us with your face. Amen.

PSALM 9:1–4, 7–10

I will praise you, O LORD, with all my heart; I will tell of all your wonders. I will be glad and rejoice in you; I will sing praise to your name, O Most High.

My enemies turn back; they stumble and perish before you. For you have upheld my right and my cause; you have sat on your throne, judging righteously.

The LORD reigns forever; he has established his throne for judgment. He will judge the world in righteousness; he will govern the peoples with justice. The LORD is a refuge for the oppressed, a stronghold in times of trouble. Those who know your name will trust in you, for you, LORD, have never forsaken those who seek you.

SPACE FOR REFLECTION

CLOSING PRAYERS

Let your mercy, O Lord, be upon us.
As we have hoped in you.

Lord, have mercy.
Christ, have mercy.
Lord, have mercy.

Our Father, who art in heaven. . . .

Lord, hear my prayer.
And let my cry come unto you.
Let us bless the Lord.
Thanks be to God.
May divine help always be with us.
And with those who are absent from us.
Amen.

VESPERS

Tuesday
Week 1

O God, come to my assistance.
O Lord, make haste to help me.

OPENING PRAYER

O great Creator of the earth, cleanse the wounds of our souls with the freshness of your grace, destroy wrong impulses, and let us be filled with your good things. Amen.

PSALM 33:1–12

Sing joyfully to the LORD, you righteous; it is fitting for the upright to praise him. Praise the LORD with the harp; make music to him on the ten-stringed lyre. Sing to him a new song; play skillfully, and shout for joy.

For the word of the LORD is right and true; he is faithful in all he does. The LORD loves righteousness and justice; the earth is full of his unfailing love.

By the word of the LORD were the heavens made, their starry host by the breath of his mouth. He gathers the waters of the sea into jars ; he puts the deep into storehouses.

Let all the earth fear the LORD; let all the people of the world revere him. For he spoke, and it came to be; he commanded, and it stood firm.

The LORD foils the plans of the nations; he thwarts the purposes of the peoples. But the plans of the LORD stand firm forever, the purposes of his heart through all generations. Blessed is the nation whose God is the LORD, the people he chose for his inheritance.

GOSPEL READING
John 1:10–13

He was in the world, and though the world was made through him, the world did not recognize him. He came to that which was his own, but his own did not receive him. Yet to all who received him, to those who believed in his name, he gave the right to become children of God—children born not of natural descent, nor of human decision or a husband's will, but born of God.

SPACE FOR REFLECTION

CLOSING PRAYERS
Lord, have mercy.
Christ, have mercy.
Lord, have mercy.

Our Father, who art in heaven. . . .

Lord, hear my prayer.
And let my cry come unto you.

COLLECT

O living and eternal God, you are more ready to give than we to ask. Grant us a new vision of yourself, that seeing you as you are, we may desire you, and desiring you, may surrender our lives to you. We ask this through our Lord Jesus Christ your Son. Amen.

Lord, hear my prayer.
And let my cry come unto you.
Let us bless the Lord.
Thanks be to God.

May the souls of the faithful
by the mercy of God rest in peace.
Amen.
May divine help always be with us.
And with those who are absent from us.
Amen.

MORNING PRAYER

Wednesday
Week 1

O Lord, open my lips.
And my mouth will proclaim your praise.

OPENING PRAYER

To you, O Christ, King most loving, and to the Father be glory with the Spirit, the Paraclete, for everlasting ages. Amen.

PSALM 67

May God be gracious to us and bless us and make his face shine upon us, that your ways may be known on earth, your salvation among all nations.

May the peoples praise you, O God; may all the peoples praise you. May the nations be glad and sing for joy, for you rule the peoples justly and guide the nations of the earth. May the peoples praise you, O God; may all the peoples praise you.

Then the land will yield its harvest, and God, our God, will bless us. God will bless us, and all the ends of the earth will fear him.

READING
Frederica Mathewes-Green

The starting point for the early church was this awareness of the abyss of sin inside each person. God, who is all charity and light, wants to make us perfect as he is perfect, shot through with his radiance. The first step in our healing, then, is not being comforted. It is taking a hard look at the cleansing that needs to be done.

SPACE FOR REFLECTION

CLOSING PRAYERS
Lord, have mercy.
Christ, have mercy.
Lord, have mercy.

Our Father, who art in heaven. . . .

Lord, hear my prayer.
And let my cry come unto you.

COLLECT

Gracious Father in heaven, you alone are the source of our peace and look mercifully upon your people in their moments of need. Bring us to the dignity which distinguishes the poor in spirit, and show us how great is the call to serve. We ask this through our Lord Jesus Christ your Son, who lives and reigns with you and the Holy Spirit, one God forever and ever. Amen.

Lord, hear my prayer.
And let my cry come unto you.
Let us bless the Lord.
Thanks be to God.

May the souls of the faithful
by the mercy of God rest in peace.
Amen.
May divine help always be with us.
And with those who are absent from us.
Amen.

MIDDAY SERVICE

Wednesday
Week 1

O God, come to my assistance.
O Lord, make haste to help me.

OPENING PRAYER

Jesus, Lord God and Creator of all things, be yourself our joy, who are the future prize. May our glory be in you always, through all the ages. Amen.

PSALM 23

The LORD is my shepherd, I shall not be in want. He makes me lie down in green pastures, he leads me beside quiet waters, he restores my soul. He guides me in paths of righteousness for his name's sake.

Even though I walk through the valley of the shadow of death, I will fear no evil, for you are with me; your rod and your staff, they comfort me.

You prepare a table before me in the presence of my enemies. You anoint my head with oil; my cup overflows. Surely goodness

and love will follow me all the days of my life,
and I will dwell in the house of the LORD
forever.

SPACE FOR REFLECTION

CLOSING PRAYERS
Let your mercy, O Lord, be upon us.
As we have hoped in you.

Lord, have mercy.
Christ, have mercy.
Lord, have mercy.

Our Father, who art in heaven. . . .

Lord, hear my prayer.
And let my cry come unto you.
Let us bless the Lord.
Thanks be to God.
May divine help always be with us.
And with those who are absent from us.
Amen.

VESPERS

Wednesday
Week 1

O God, come to my assistance.
O Lord, make haste to help me.

OPENING PRAYER

Most holy God of heaven, you who paint the shining center of the sky with the brightness of fire, illumine our hearts, banish sordid things, release the chain of guilt, and make void our crimes. Amen.

PSALM 15

LORD, who may dwell in your sanctuary? Who may live on your holy hill?

He whose walk is blameless and who does what is righteous, who speaks the truth from his heart and has no slander on his tongue, who does his neighbor no wrong and casts no slur on his fellowman, who despises a vile man but honors those who fear the LORD, who keeps his oath even when it hurts, who lends his money without usury and does not accept a bribe against the innocent. He who does these things will never be shaken.

GOSPEL READING
John 1:14–18

The Word became flesh and made his dwelling among us. We have seen his glory, the glory of the One and Only, who came from the Father, full of grace and truth.

John testifies concerning him. He cries out, saying, "This was he of whom I said, 'He who comes after me has surpassed me because he was before me.'" From the fullness of his grace we have all received one blessing after another. For the law was given through Moses; grace and truth came through Jesus Christ. No one has ever seen God, but God the One and Only, who is at the Father's side, has made him known.

SPACE FOR REFLECTION

CLOSING PRAYERS
Lord, have mercy.
Christ, have mercy.
Lord, have mercy.

Our Father, who art in heaven. . . .

Lord, hear my prayer.
And let my cry come unto you.

COLLECT

Gracious Father in heaven, you alone are the source of our peace and look mercifully upon your people in their moments of need. Bring us to the dignity which distinguishes the poor in spirit, and show us how great is the call to serve. We ask this through our Lord Jesus Christ your Son, who lives and reigns with you and the Holy Spirit, one God forever and ever. Amen.

Lord, hear my prayer.
And let my cry come unto you.
Let us bless the Lord.
Thanks be to God.

May the souls of the faithful
by the mercy of God rest in peace.
Amen.
May divine help always be with us.
And with those who are absent from us.
Amen.

MORNING PRAYER

Thursday
Week 1

O Lord, open my lips.
And my mouth will proclaim your praise.

OPENING PRAYER
Behold, the fiery sun is rising; may blindness at last depart—let us speak nothing under-handed, let us consider nothing dark. To God the Father be glory, and to his only Son, with the Spirit, the Paraclete, for everlasting ages. Amen.

PSALM 100
Shout for joy to the LORD, all the earth. Worship the LORD with gladness; come before him with joyful songs. Know that the LORD is God. It is he who made us, and we are his; we are his people, the sheep of his pasture.

Enter his gates with thanksgiving and his courts with praise; give thanks to him and praise his name. For the LORD is good and his love endures forever; his faithfulness continues through all generations.

READING

Augustine of Hippo

You awake us to delight in your praise; for you made us for yourself, and our hearts are restless until they rest in you.

SPACE FOR REFLECTION

CLOSING PRAYERS

Lord, have mercy.
Christ, have mercy.
Lord, have mercy.

Our Father, who art in heaven. . . .

Lord, hear my prayer.
And let my cry come unto you.

COLLECT

Lord, our eternal God, you alone are worthy of our highest praise. Help us to love you above all things, that we might serve our brothers and sisters with a love that is worthy of you. We ask this through our Lord Jesus Christ your Son, who lives and reigns with you and the Holy Spirit, one God forever and ever. Amen.

Lord, hear my prayer.
And let my cry come unto you.
Let us bless the Lord.
Thanks be to God.

May the souls of the faithful
by the mercy of God rest in peace.
Amen.
May divine help always be with us.
And with those who are absent from us.
Amen.

MIDDAY SERVICE

Thursday
Week 1

O God, come to my assistance.
O Lord, make haste to help me.

OPENING PRAYER

Come, Creator Spirit, Paraclete, gift of God most high, visit the souls of your people, and fill with supernal grace the hearts which you created. Amen.

PSALM 16:1–3, 5–11

Keep me safe, O God, for in you I take refuge. I said to the LORD, "You are my Lord; apart from you I have no good thing." As for the saints who are in the land, they are the glorious ones in whom is all my delight.

LORD, you have assigned me my portion and my cup; you have made my lot secure. The boundary lines have fallen for me in pleasant places; surely I have a delightful inheritance.

I will praise the LORD, who counsels me; even at night my heart instructs me.

I have set the LORD always before me. Because he is at my right hand, I will not be shaken.

Therefore my heart is glad and my tongue rejoices; my body also will rest secure, because you will not abandon me to the grave, nor will you let your Holy One see decay.

You have made known to me the path of life; you will fill me with joy in your presence, with eternal pleasures at your right hand.

SPACE FOR REFLECTION

CLOSING PRAYERS

Let your mercy, O Lord, be upon us.
As we have hoped in you.

Lord, have mercy.
Christ, have mercy.
Lord, have mercy.

Our Father, who art in heaven. . . .

Lord, hear my prayer.
And let my cry come unto you.
Let us bless the Lord.
Thanks be to God.
May divine help always be with us.
And with those who are absent from us.
Amen.

VESPERS

Thursday
Week 1

O God, come to my assistance.
O Lord, make haste to help me.

OPENING PRAYER

O God of great power, you have rescued us
from error and from the weariness of death.
We give you thanks and praise. Amen.

PSALM 46:1–3, 6–11

God is our refuge and strength, an ever-present
help in trouble. Therefore we will not fear,
though the earth give way and the mountains
fall into the heart of the sea, though its waters
roar and foam and the mountains quake with
their surging.

Nations are in uproar, kingdoms fall; he
lifts his voice, the earth melts.

The LORD Almighty is with us; the God
of Jacob is our fortress.

Come and see the works of the LORD,
the desolations he has brought on the earth.
He makes wars cease to the ends of the earth;
he breaks the bow and shatters the spear, he
burns the shields with fire.

"Be still, and know that I am God; I will be exalted among the nations, I will be exalted in the earth."

The LORD Almighty is with us; the God of Jacob is our fortress.

GOSPEL READING
John 1:29, 32–34

The next day John saw Jesus coming toward him and said, "Look, the Lamb of God, who takes away the sin of the world!"

Then John gave this testimony: "I saw the Spirit come down from heaven as a dove and remain on him. I would not have known him, except that the one who sent me to baptize with water told me, 'The man on whom you see the Spirit come down and remain is he who will baptize with the Holy Spirit.' I have seen and I testify that this is the Son of God."

SPACE FOR REFLECTION

CLOSING PRAYERS
Lord, have mercy.
Christ, have mercy.
Lord, have mercy.

Our Father, who art in heaven. . . .

Lord, hear my prayer.
And let my cry come unto you.

COLLECT

Lord, our eternal God, you alone are worthy of our highest praise. Help us to love you above all things, that we might serve our brothers and sisters with a love that is worthy of you. We ask this through our Lord Jesus Christ your Son, who lives and reigns with you and the Holy Spirit, one God forever and ever. Amen.

Lord, hear my prayer.
And let my cry come unto you.
Let us bless the Lord.
Thanks be to God.

May the souls of the faithful
by the mercy of God rest in peace.
Amen.
May divine help always be with us.
And with those who are absent from us.
Amen.

MORNING PRAYER

Friday
Week 1

O Lord, open my lips.
And my mouth will proclaim your praise.

OPENING PRAYER

O eternal Glory of heaven, blessed Hope of mortals, give your right hand to those who are getting up; let the soul arise sober and, ardent in praise, returning thanks to you. Amen.

PSALM 122

I rejoiced with those who said to me, "Let us go to the house of the LORD." Our feet are standing in your gates, O Jerusalem.

Jerusalem is built like a city that is closely compacted together. That is where the tribes go up, the tribes of the LORD, to praise the name of the LORD according to the statute given to Israel. There the thrones for judgment stand, the thrones of the house of David.

Pray for the peace of Jerusalem: "May those who love you be secure. May there be peace within your walls and security within your citadels." For the sake of my brothers and friends, I will say, "Peace be within you." For the sake of the house of the LORD our God, I will seek your prosperity.

READING
Linette Martin

Silence is a form of prayer. But it leads naturally to other forms of prayer. Think about simply growing toward prayer from that place of silence to a new place, as gently and naturally as the growing of a plant.

SPACE FOR REFLECTION

CLOSING PRAYERS

Lord, have mercy.
Christ, have mercy.
Lord, have mercy.

Our Father, who art in heaven. . . .

Lord, hear my prayer.
And let my cry come unto you.

COLLECT

Lord of all, the Alpha and Omega, you are the beginning and end of every good desire. May all we do be done for love of you and brought to completion with your almighty help. We ask this through our Lord Jesus Christ your Son. Amen.

Lord, hear my prayer.
And let my cry come unto you.
Let us bless the Lord.
Thanks be to God.

May the souls of the faithful
by the mercy of God rest in peace.
Amen.
May divine help always be with us.
And with those who are absent from us.
Amen.

MIDDAY SERVICE

Friday
Week 1

O God, come to my assistance.
O Lord, make haste to help me.

OPENING PRAYER

Come, Holy Spirit, kindle light for our senses, pour out love in our hearts, and undergird with perpetual strength the weaknesses of our body. Amen.

PSALM 17:1–9

Hear, O LORD, my righteous plea; listen to my cry. Give ear to my prayer—it does not rise from deceitful lips. May my vindication come from you; may your eyes see what is right. Though you probe my heart and examine me at night, though you test me, you will find nothing; I have resolved that my mouth will not sin. As for the deeds of men—by the word of your lips I have kept myself from the ways of the violent. My steps have held to your paths; my feet have not slipped.

I call on you, O God, for you will answer me; give ear to me and hear my prayer. Show the wonder of your great love, you who save by your right hand those who take refuge in you from their foes. Keep me as the apple of your eye; hide me in the shadow of your wings from the wicked who assail me, from my mortal enemies who surround me.

SPACE FOR REFLECTION

CLOSING PRAYERS
Let your mercy, O Lord, be upon us.
As we have hoped in you.

Lord, have mercy.
Christ, have mercy.
Lord, have mercy.

Our Father, who art in heaven. . . .

Lord, hear my prayer.
And let my cry come unto you.
Let us bless the Lord.
Thanks be to God.
May divine help always be with us.
And with those who are absent from us.
Amen.

VESPERS

Friday
Week 1

O God, come to my assistance.
O Lord, make haste to help me.

OPENING PRAYER

O God, Maker of all mankind, give the rewards of joy, grant the gifts of graces, dissolve the chains of quarreling, and bind fast the agreements of peace. Amen.

PSALM 48:1–3, 8–14

Great is the LORD, and most worthy of praise, in the city of our God, his holy mountain. It is beautiful in its loftiness, the joy of the whole earth. Like the utmost heights of Zaphon is Mount Zion, the city of the Great King. God is in her citadels; he has shown himself to be her fortress.

As we have heard, so have we seen in the city of the LORD Almighty, in the city of our God: God makes her secure forever.

Within your temple, O God, we meditate on your unfailing love. Like your name, O God, your praise reaches to the ends of the earth; your right hand is filled with righteousness.

Mount Zion rejoices, the villages of Judah are glad because of your judgments.

Walk about Zion, go around her, count her towers, consider well her ramparts, view her citadels, that you may tell of them to the next generation. For this God is our God for ever and ever; he will be our guide even to the end.

GOSPEL READING
John 3:16–18

"For God so loved the world that he gave his one and only Son, that whoever believes in him shall not perish but have eternal life. For God did not send his Son into the world to condemn the world, but to save the world through him. Whoever believes in him is not condemned, but whoever does not believe stands condemned already because he has not believed in the name of God's one and only Son."

SPACE FOR REFLECTION

CLOSING PRAYERS
Lord, have mercy.
Christ, have mercy.
Lord, have mercy.

Our Father, who art in heaven. . . .

Lord, hear my prayer.
And let my cry come unto you.

COLLECT

Lord of all, the Alpha and Omega, you are the beginning and end of every good desire. May all we do be done for love of you and brought to completion with your almighty help. We pray this in the name of our Lord and Savior Jesus Christ. Amen.

Lord, hear my prayer.
And let my cry come unto you.
Let us bless the Lord.
Thanks be to God.

May the souls of the faithful
by the mercy of God rest in peace.
Amen.
May divine help always be with us.
And with those who are absent from us.
Amen.

MORNING PRAYER

Saturday
Week 1

O Lord, open my lips.
And my mouth will proclaim your praise.

OPENING PRAYER

O Light, shine on our senses and dispel the sleep of our soul. To you before all else may our voice resound, and let us pay our vows to you. Amen.

PSALM 30

I will exalt you, O LORD, for you lifted me out of the depths and did not let my enemies gloat over me. O LORD my God, I called to you for help and you healed me. O LORD, you brought me up from the grave; you spared me from going down into the pit. Sing to the LORD, you saints of his; praise his holy name. For his anger lasts only a moment, but his favor lasts a lifetime; weeping may remain for a night, but rejoicing comes in the morning.

When I felt secure, I said, "I will never be shaken." O LORD, when you favored me, you made my mountain stand firm; but when you hid your face, I was dismayed.

To you, O LORD, I called; to the LORD I cried for mercy: "What gain is there in my destruction, in my going down into the pit? Will the dust praise you? Will it proclaim your faithfulness? Hear, O LORD, and be merciful to me; O LORD, be my help."

You turned my wailing into dancing; you removed my sackcloth and clothed me with joy, that my heart may sing to you and not be silent. O LORD my God, I will give you thanks forever.

READING
Daniel Homan, O.S.B., and Lonni Collins Pratt
The Mystery of the other is a reflection of God's mystery as well. God is ultimately the stranger who comes to us, the stranger within, the stranger who intrudes with her neediness and her hurting. God is the stranger we never quite understand.

SPACE FOR REFLECTION

CLOSING PRAYERS
Lord, have mercy.
Christ, have mercy.
Lord, have mercy.

Our Father, who art in heaven. . . .

Lord, hear my prayer.
And let my cry come unto you.

COLLECT

Mighty Lord of heaven and earth, whose Son is the head of the church, shape and renew your people until we bear the image of Christ and show his true likeness to the world. We ask this through the same Jesus Christ your Son, who lives and reigns with you and the Holy Spirit, one God forever and ever. Amen.

Lord, hear my prayer.
And let my cry come unto you.
Let us bless the Lord.
Thanks be to God.

May the souls of the faithful
by the mercy of God rest in peace.
Amen.
May divine help always be with us.
And with those who are absent from us.
Amen.

MIDDAY
SERVICE

Saturday
Week 1

O God, come to my assistance.
O Lord, make haste to help me.

OPENING PRAYER

Grant us a wholesome life, revive our zeal and love, O Father Almighty, through Jesus Christ the Lord, who reigns with you for all time with the Holy Spirit. Amen.

PSALM 121

I lift up my eyes to the hills—where does my help come from? My help comes from the LORD, the Maker of heaven and earth. He will not let your foot slip—he who watches over you will not slumber; indeed, he who watches over Israel will neither slumber nor sleep.

The LORD watches over you—the LORD is your shade at your right hand; the sun will not harm you by day, nor the moon by night.

The LORD will keep you from all harm—he will watch over your life; the

LORD will watch over your coming and going both now and forevermore.

SPACE FOR REFLECTION

CLOSING PRAYERS
Let your mercy, O Lord, be upon us.
As we have hoped in you.

Lord, have mercy.
Christ, have mercy.
Lord, have mercy.

Our Father, who art in heaven. . . .

Lord, hear my prayer.
And let my cry come unto you.
Let us bless the Lord.
Thanks be to God.
May divine help always be with us.
And with those who are absent from us.
Amen.

VESPERS

Saturday
Week 1

O God, come to my assistance.
O Lord, make haste to help me.

OPENING PRAYER

O God, Creator of all things and Ruler of heaven, we give thanks for the day that is finished, and we pray at the start of the night. May faith not know darkness; may the night shine with faith. Amen.

PSALM 116:1, 2, 8–16

I love the LORD, for he heard my voice; the heard my cry for mercy. Because he turned his ear to me, I will call on him as long as I live.

For you, O LORD, have delivered my soul from death, my eyes from tears, my feet from stumbling, that I may walk before the LORD in the land of the living. I believed; therefore I said, "I am greatly afflicted." And in my dismay I said, "All men are liars."

How can I repay the LORD for all his goodness to me? I will lift up the cup of salvation and call on the name of the LORD. I will fulfill my vows to the LORD in the presence of all his people.

Precious in the sight of the LORD is the death of his saints. O LORD, truly I am your servant; I am your servant, the son of your maidservant; you have freed me from my chains.

GOSPEL READING
John 4:11, 13, 14

"Sir," the woman said, "you have nothing to draw with and the well is deep. Where can you get this living water?"

Jesus answered, "Everyone who drinks this water will be thirsty again, but whoever drinks the water I give him will never thirst. Indeed, the water I give him will become in him a spring of water welling up to eternal life."

SPACE FOR REFLECTION

CLOSING PRAYERS

Lord, have mercy.
Christ, have mercy.
Lord, have mercy.

Our Father, who art in heaven. . . .

Lord, hear my prayer.
And let my cry come unto you.

COLLECT

Mighty Lord of heaven and earth, whose Son is the head of the church, shape and renew your people until we bear the image of Christ and show his true likeness to the world. We ask this through our Lord Jesus Christ your Son. Amen.

Lord, hear my prayer.
And let my cry come unto you.
Let us bless the Lord.
Thanks be to God.

May the souls of the faithful
by the mercy of God rest in peace.
Amen.
May divine help always be with us.
And with those who are absent from us.
Amen.

WEEK 2

MORNING PRAYER

Sunday
Week 2

O Lord, open my lips.
And my mouth will proclaim your praise.

OPENING PRAYER

May our compassionate God drive away all
our anguish, bestow health, and give us, by
the loving-kindness of the Father, the kingdom of the heavens. Amen.

PSALM 150

Praise the LORD. Praise God in his sanctuary;
praise him in his mighty heavens. Praise
him for his acts of power; praise him for his
surpassing greatness. Praise him with the
sounding of the trumpet, praise him with the
harp and lyre, praise him with tambourine
and dancing, praise him with the strings and
flute, praise him with the clash of cymbals,
praise him with resounding cymbals.

Let everything that has breath praise the
LORD. Praise the LORD.

READING
François Fénelon

How rare it is to find a soul still enough to hear God speak! The slightest murmur of our vain desires, or of a love fixed upon itself, confounds all the words of the Spirit of God.

SPACE FOR REFLECTION

BENEDICTUS
Canticle of Zechariah: Luke 1:68–79

"Praise be to the Lord, the God of Israel, because he has come and has redeemed his people. He has raised up a horn of salvation for us in the house of his servant David (as he said through his holy prophets of long ago), salvation from our enemies and from the hand of all who hate us—to show mercy to our fathers and to remember his holy covenant, the oath he swore to our father Abraham: to rescue us from the hand of our enemies, and to enable us to serve him without fear in holiness and righteousness before him all our days.

And you, my child, will be called a prophet of the Most High; for you will go on before the Lord to prepare the way for him, to give his people the knowledge of salvation through the forgiveness of their sins, because of the tender mercy of our God, by which the rising sun will come to us from heaven to shine on those living in darkness and in the shadow of death, to guide our feet into the path of peace."

CLOSING PRAYERS

Lord, have mercy.
Christ, have mercy.
Lord, have mercy.

Our Father, who art in heaven. . . .

Lord, hear my prayer.
And let my cry come unto you.

COLLECT

Lord our eternal God, you increase and multiply your faithful by the abundant gift of your grace. Look now on your chosen people, and clothe forever in the garment of eternal life all who in baptism have been reborn. We ask this through our Lord Jesus Christ your Son, who lives and reigns with you and the Holy Spirit, one God forever and ever. Amen.

Lord, hear my prayer.
And let my cry come unto you.
Let us bless the Lord.
Thanks be to God.

May the souls of the faithful
by the mercy of God rest in peace.
Amen.
May divine help always be with us.
And with those who are absent from us.
Amen.

MIDDAY
SERVICE

Sunday
Week 2

O God, come to my assistance.
O Lord, make haste to help me.

OPENING PRAYER

Mighty Ruler, true God, you who regulate the functions of all things and provide the morning its splendor, the midday its heat. Extinguish the flames of quarrels, take away harmful passions, grant healing of body and true peace of heart. Amen.

PSALM 119:1–8

Blessed are they whose ways are blameless, who walk according to the law of the LORD. Blessed are they who keep his statutes and seek him with all their heart. They do nothing wrong; they walk in his ways. You have laid down precepts that are to be fully obeyed. Oh, that my ways were steadfast in obeying your decrees! Then I would not be put to shame when I consider all your commands. I will praise you with an upright heart as I learn

your righteous laws. I will obey your decrees;
do not utterly forsake me.

SPACE FOR REFLECTION

CLOSING PRAYERS
Let your mercy, O Lord, be upon us.
As we have hoped in you.

Lord, have mercy.
Christ, have mercy.
Lord, have mercy.

Our Father, who art in heaven. . . .

Lord, hear my prayer.
And let my cry come unto you.
Let us bless the Lord.
Thanks be to God.
May divine help always be with us.
And with those who are absent from us.
Amen.

VESPERS

Sunday
Week 2

O God, come to my assistance.
O Lord, make haste to help me.

OPENING PRAYER

O Light, blessed Trinity and perfect Unity, already the fiery sun is receding; pour light into our hearts. Amen.

PSALM 133, 134

How good and pleasant it is when brothers live together in unity! It is like precious oil poured on the head, running down on the beard, running down on Aaron's beard, down upon the collar of his robes. It is as if the dew of Hermon were falling on Mount Zion. For there the LORD bestows his blessing, even life forevermore.

Praise the LORD, all you servants of the LORD who minister by night in the house of the LORD. Lift up your hands in the sanctuary and praise the LORD. May the LORD, the Maker of heaven and earth, bless you from Zion.

GOSPEL READING
John 5:19, 21

Jesus gave them this answer: "I tell you the truth, the Son can do nothing by himself; he can do only what he sees his Father doing, because whatever the Father does, the Son also does. . . . For just as the Father raises the dead and gives life, even so the Son gives life to whom he is pleased to give it."

SPACE FOR REFLECTION

MAGNIFICAT
The Canticle of Mary: Luke 1:46b–55

"My soul glorifies the Lord and my spirit rejoices in God my Savior, for he has been mindful of the humble state of his servant. From now on all generations will call me blessed, for the Mighty One has done great things for me—holy is his name. His mercy extends to those who fear him, from generation to generation. He has performed mighty deeds with his arm; he has scattered those who are proud in their inmost thoughts. He has brought down rulers from their thrones but has lifted up the humble. He has filled the hungry with good things but has sent the rich away empty. He has helped his servant Israel, remembering to be merciful to

Abraham and his descendants forever, even as he said to our fathers."

CLOSING PRAYERS
Lord, have mercy.
Christ, have mercy.
Lord, have mercy.

Our Father, who art in heaven. . . .

Lord, hear my prayer.
And let my cry come unto you.

COLLECT
Lord our eternal God, you increase and multiply your faithful by the abundant gift of your grace. Look now on your chosen people, and clothe forever in the garment of eternal life all who in baptism have been reborn. We ask this through our Lord Jesus Christ your Son, who lives and reigns with you and the Holy Spirit, one God forever and ever. Amen.

Lord, hear my prayer.
And let my cry come unto you.
Let us bless the Lord.
Thanks be to God.

May the souls of the faithful
by the mercy of God rest in peace.
Amen.
May divine help always be with us.
And with those who are absent from us.
Amen.

MORNING PRAYER

Monday
Week 2

O Lord, open my lips.
And my mouth will proclaim your praise.

OPENING PRAYER

Lord Jesus, Splendor of the Father's glory, O
true Sun, descend, sparkling with uninterrupted brightness; O radiance of the Holy
Spirit, pour in upon our senses. Amen.

PSALM 146

Praise the LORD. Praise the LORD, O my soul.
I will praise the LORD all my life; I will sing
praise to my God as long as I live.

Do not put your trust in princes, in
mortal men, who cannot save. When their
spirit departs, they return to the ground; on
that very day their plans come to nothing.

Blessed is he whose help is the God of
Jacob, whose hope is in the LORD his God,
the Maker of heaven and earth, the sea, and
everything in them—the LORD, who remains
faithful forever. He upholds the cause of the

oppressed and gives food to the hungry. The LORD sets prisoners free, the LORD gives sight to the blind, the LORD lifts up those who are bowed down, the LORD loves the righteous. The LORD watches over the alien and sustains the fatherless and the widow, but he frustrates the ways of the wicked.

The LORD reigns forever, your God, O Zion, for all generations. Praise the LORD.

READING
Cardinal Basil Hume

A mystery is a truth which lies beyond us. It can be entered into, explored, inhabited even; but it can never be exhausted or fathomed. Our age dislikes intensely the idea of mystery, because it directly exposes our limitations.

SPACE FOR REFLECTION

CLOSING PRAYERS
Lord, have mercy.
Christ, have mercy.
Lord, have mercy.

Our Father, who art in heaven. . . .

Lord, hear my prayer.
And let my cry come unto you.

COLLECT

Heavenly and merciful Father, it is from you that redemption comes to us, your adopted children. Look with favor on the family you love. Give true freedom to all who believe in Christ, and bring us all alike to our eternal heritage. We pray this in the name of our Lord and Savior, Jesus Christ your Son. Amen.

Lord, hear my prayer.
And let my cry come unto you.
Let us bless the Lord.
Thanks be to God.

May the souls of the faithful
by the mercy of God rest in peace.
Amen.
May divine help always be with us.
And with those who are absent from us.
Amen.

MIDDAY SERVICE

Monday
Week 2

O God, come to my assistance.
O Lord, make haste to help me.

OPENING PRAYER
O Christ, you are the Light, the Splendor of the Father, and the eternal Hope of all things. Listen to the prayers which your servants throughout the world pour forth. Amen.

PSALM 119:9–16
How can a young man keep his way pure? By living according to your word. I seek you with all my heart; do not let me stray from your commands. I have hidden your word in my heart that I might not sin against you. Praise be to you, O LORD; teach me your decrees. With my lips I recount all the laws that come from your mouth. I rejoice in following your statutes as one rejoices in great riches. I meditate on your precepts and consider your ways. I delight in your decrees; I will not neglect your word.

SPACE FOR REFLECTION

CLOSING PRAYERS

Let your mercy, O Lord, be upon us.
As we have hoped in you.

Lord, have mercy.
Christ, have mercy.
Lord, have mercy.

Our Father, who art in heaven. . . .

Lord, hear my prayer.
And let my cry come unto you.
Let us bless the Lord.
Thanks be to God.
May divine help always be with us.
And with those who are absent from us.
Amen.

VESPERS

Monday
Week 2

O God, come to my assistance.
O Lord, make haste to help me.

OPENING PRAYER

Pour into us now, O most loving One, the gift of eternal grace, so that, by the misfortunes of new deception, old error may not destroy us. Amen.

PSALM 115:1–9, 14, 15

Not to us, O LORD, not to us but to your name be the glory, because of your love and faithfulness. Why do the nations say, "Where is their God?" Our God is in heaven; he does whatever pleases him. But their idols are silver and gold, made by the hands of men. They have mouths, but cannot speak, eyes, but they cannot see; they have ears, but cannot hear, noses, but they cannot smell; they have hands, but cannot feel, feet, but they cannot walk; nor can they utter a sound with their throats. Those who make them will be like them, and so will all who trust in them.

O house of Israel, trust in the LORD—he is their help and shield.

May the LORD make you increase, both you and your children. May you be blessed by the LORD, the Maker of heaven and earth.

GOSPEL READING
John 5:24–26

"I tell you the truth, whoever hears my word and believes him who sent me has eternal life and will not be condemned; he has crossed over from death to life. I tell you the truth, a time is coming and has now come when the dead will hear the voice of the Son of God and those who hear will live. For as the Father has life in himself, so he has granted the Son to have life in himself."

SPACE FOR REFLECTION

CLOSING PRAYERS

Lord, have mercy.
Christ, have mercy.
Lord, have mercy.

Our Father, who art in heaven. . . .

Lord, hear my prayer.
And let my cry come unto you.

COLLECT

Heavenly and merciful Father, it is from you that redemption comes to us, your adopted children. Look with favor on the family you love. Give true freedom to all who believe in Christ, and bring us all alike to our eternal heritage. We ask this through the same Jesus Christ your Son, who lives and reigns with you and the Holy Spirit, one God, forever and ever. Amen.

Lord, hear my prayer.
And let my cry come unto you.
Let us bless the Lord.
Thanks be to God.

May the souls of the faithful
by the mercy of God rest in peace.
Amen.
May divine help always be with us.
And with those who are absent from us.
Amen.

MORNING PRAYER

Tuesday
Week 2

O Lord, open my lips.
And my mouth will proclaim your praise.

OPENING PRAYER
O Christ, dispel sleep, break the chains of night, release long-standing sin, and pour in new light. Amen.

PSALM 147:1–11
Praise the LORD. How good it is to sing praises to our God, how pleasant and fitting to praise him! The LORD builds up Jerusalem; he gathers the exiles of Israel. He heals the brokenhearted and binds up their wounds. He determines the number of the stars and calls them each by name. Great is our Lord and mighty in power; his understanding has no limit. The LORD sustains the humble but casts the wicked to the ground.

Sing to the LORD with thanksgiving; make music to our God on the harp. He covers the sky with clouds; he supplies the earth with rain and makes grass grow on the hills. He provides food for the cattle and for the young ravens when they call.

His pleasure is not in the strength of the horse, nor his delight in the legs of a man; the LORD delights in those who fear him, who put their hope in his unfailing love.

READING
Thomas à Kempis

All men naturally desire knowledge; but what good is knowledge without the fear of God? Surely a humble peasant who fears God is better than a proud philosopher who, neglecting his own soul, occupies himself in studying the course of the stars.

SPACE FOR REFLECTION

CLOSING PRAYERS
Lord, have mercy.
Christ, have mercy.
Lord, have mercy.

Our Father, who art in heaven. . . .

Lord, hear my prayer.
And let my cry come unto you.

COLLECT

Heavenly Lord of love, in your goodness you have opened our eyes to your light. So fill our hearts with your glory that we may always acknowledge Jesus as Savior, and hold fast to his word in sincerity and truth. We ask this through the same Jesus Christ your Son, who lives and reigns with you and the Holy Spirit, one God, forever and ever. Amen.

Lord, hear my prayer.
And let my cry come unto you.
Let us bless the Lord.
Thanks be to God.

May the souls of the faithful
by the mercy of God rest in peace.
Amen.
May divine help always be with us.
And with those who are absent from us.
Amen.

MIDDAY SERVICE

Tuesday
Week 2

O God, come to my assistance.
O Lord, make haste to help me.

OPENING PRAYER

O Jesus, our redemption, love, and desire, may your love constrain you to pass over our evils, sparing us, and having answered our prayer, may you satisfy us with your face. Amen.

PSALM 119:17–24

Do good to your servant, and I will live; I will obey your word. Open my eyes that I may see wonderful things in your law. I am a stranger on earth; do not hide your commands from me. My soul is consumed with longing for your laws at all times. You rebuke the arrogant, who are cursed and who stray from your commands. Remove from me scorn and contempt, for I keep your statutes. Though rulers sit together and slander me, your servant will meditate on your decrees.

Your statutes are my delight; they are my counselors.

SPACE FOR REFLECTION

CLOSING PRAYERS
Let your mercy, O Lord, be upon us.
As we have hoped in you.

Lord, have mercy.
Christ, have mercy.
Lord, have mercy.

Our Father, who art in heaven. . . .

Lord, hear my prayer.
And let my cry come unto you.
Let us bless the Lord.
Thanks be to God.
May divine help always be with us.
And with those who are absent from us.
Amen.

VESPERS

Tuesday
Week 2

O God, come to my assistance.
O Lord, make haste to help me.

OPENING PRAYER
O great Creator of the earth, cleanse the wounds of our souls with the freshness of your grace, destroy wrong impulses, and let us be filled with your good things. Amen.

PSALM 68:4–10
Sing to God, sing praise to his name, extol him who rides on the clouds—his name is the LORD—and rejoice before him. A father to the fatherless, a defender of widows, is God in his holy dwelling. God sets the lonely in families, he leads forth the prisoners with singing; but the rebellious live in a sunscorched land.

When you went out before your people, O God, when you marched through the wasteland, the earth shook, the heavens poured down rain, before God, the One of Sinai, before God, the God of Israel. You gave abundant showers, O God; you refreshed your weary inheritance. Your people settled in it, and from your bounty, O God, you provided for the poor.

GOSPEL READING
John 6:39, 40
"And this is the will of him who sent me, that I shall lose none of all that he has given me, but raise them up on the last day. For my Father's will is that everyone who looks to the Son and believes in him shall have eternal life, and I will raise him up at the last day."

SPACE FOR REFLECTION

CLOSING PRAYERS
Lord, have mercy.
Christ, have mercy.
Lord, have mercy.

Our Father, who art in heaven. . . .

Lord, hear my prayer.
And let my cry come unto you.

COLLECT
Heavenly Lord of love, in your goodness you have opened our eyes to your light. So fill our hearts with your glory that we may always acknowledge Jesus as Savior, and hold fast to

his word in sincerity and truth. We ask this through our Lord Jesus Christ your Son. Amen.

Lord, hear my prayer.
And let my cry come unto you.
Let us bless the Lord.
Thanks be to God.

May the souls of the faithful
by the mercy of God rest in peace.
Amen.
May divine help always be with us.
And with those who are absent from us.
Amen.

MORNING PRAYER

Wednesday
Week 2

O Lord, open my lips.
And my mouth will proclaim your praise.

OPENING PRAYER
To you, O Christ, King most loving, and to the Father be glory with the Spirit, the Paraclete, for everlasting ages. Amen.

PSALM 147:12–20
Extol the LORD, O Jerusalem; praise your God, O Zion, for he strengthens the bars of your gates and blesses your people within you. He grants peace to your borders and satisfies you with the finest of wheat.

He sends his command to the earth; his word runs swiftly. He spreads the snow like wool and scatters the frost like ashes. He hurls down his hail like pebbles. Who can withstand his icy blast? He sends his word and melts them; he stirs up his breezes, and the waters flow.

He has revealed his word to Jacob, his laws and decrees to Israel. He has done this for no other nation; they do not know his laws. Praise the LORD.

READING
Hal M. Helms

Have no fear for tomorrow, my child. Tomorrow will hold only what I bring or allow in your life. All your tomorrows are in my hand. I am the Lord of the years.

SPACE FOR REFLECTION

CLOSING PRAYERS
Lord, have mercy.
Christ, have mercy.
Lord, have mercy.

Our Father, who art in heaven. . . .

Lord, hear my prayer.
And let my cry come unto you.

COLLECT
Almighty, ever-living God, you are our heavenly Father. Grant that we, your adopted children by water and the Spirit, may continue steadfast in your love and be brought at last to live with you on high. We ask this through

our Lord Jesus Christ your Son, who lives and reigns with you and the Holy Spirit, one God forever and ever. Amen.

Lord, hear my prayer.
And let my cry come unto you.
Let us bless the Lord.
Thanks be to God.

May the souls of the faithful
by the mercy of God rest in peace.
Amen.
May divine help always be with us.
And with those who are absent from us.
Amen.

MIDDAY SERVICE

Wednesday
Week 2

O God, come to my assistance.
O Lord, make haste to help me.

OPENING PRAYER

Jesus, Lord God and Creator of all things, be yourself our joy, you who are the future prize. May our glory be in you always, through all the ages. Amen.

PSALM 119:25–32

I am laid low in the dust; preserve my life according to your word. I recounted my ways and you answered me; teach me your decrees. Let me understand the teaching of your precepts; then I will meditate on your wonders. My soul is weary with sorrow; strengthen me according to your word. Keep me from deceitful ways; be gracious to me through your law. I have chosen the way of truth; I have set my heart on your laws. I hold fast to your statutes, O LORD; do not let me be

put to shame. I run in the path of your
commands, for you have set my heart free.

SPACE FOR REFLECTION

CLOSING PRAYERS
Let your mercy, O Lord, be upon us.
As we have hoped in you.

Lord, have mercy.
Christ, have mercy.
Lord, have mercy.

Our Father, who art in heaven. . . .

Lord, hear my prayer.
And let my cry come unto you.
Let us bless the Lord.
Thanks be to God.
May divine help always be with us.
And with those who are absent from us.
Amen.

VESPERS

Wednesday
Week 2

O God, come to my assistance.
O Lord, make haste to help me.

OPENING PRAYER

Most holy God of heaven, you who paint the shining center of the sky with the brightness of fire, illumine our hearts, banish sordid things, release the chain of guilt, and make void our crimes. Amen.

PSALM 62:1–8

My soul finds rest in God alone; my salvation comes from him. He alone is my rock and my salvation; he is my fortress, I will never be shaken.

How long will you assault a man? Would all of you throw him down—this leaning wall, this tottering fence? They fully intend to topple him from his lofty place; they take delight in lies. With their mouths they bless, but in their hearts they curse.

Find rest, O my soul, in God alone; my hope comes from him. He alone is my rock and my salvation; he is my fortress, I will not be shaken. My salvation and my honor depend on God ; he is my mighty rock, my refuge. Trust in him at all times, O people; pour out your hearts to him, for God is our refuge.

GOSPEL READING
John 7:37–39

On the last and greatest day of the Feast, Jesus stood and said in a loud voice, "If anyone is thirsty, let him come to me and drink. Whoever believes in me, as the Scripture has said, streams of living water will flow from within him." By this he meant the Spirit, whom those who believed in him were later to receive. Up to that time, the Spirit had not been given, since Jesus had not yet been glorified.

SPACE FOR REFLECTION

CLOSING PRAYERS
Lord, have mercy.
Christ, have mercy.
Lord, have mercy.

Our Father, who art in heaven. . . .

Lord, hear my prayer.
And let my cry come unto you.

COLLECT

Almighty, ever-living God, you are our heavenly Father. Grant that we, your adopted children by water and the Spirit, may continue steadfast in your love and be brought at last to live with you on high. We pray this in the name of our Lord and Savior Jesus Christ. Amen.

Lord, hear my prayer.
And let my cry come unto you.
Let us bless the Lord.
Thanks be to God.

May the souls of the faithful
by the mercy of God rest in peace.
Amen.
May divine help always be with us.
And with those who are absent from us.
Amen.

MORNING PRAYER

Thursday
Week 2

O Lord, open my lips.
And my mouth will proclaim your praise.

OPENING PRAYER

Behold, the fiery sun is rising; may blindness at last depart—let us speak nothing underhanded, let us consider nothing dark. To God the Father be glory, and to his only Son, with the Spirit, the Paraclete, for everlasting ages. Amen.

PSALM 148:1–6

Praise the LORD. Praise the LORD from the heavens, praise him in the heights above. Praise him, all his angels, praise him, all his heavenly hosts. Praise him, sun and moon, praise him, all you shining stars. Praise him, you highest heavens and you waters above the skies. Let them praise the name of the LORD, for he commanded and they were created. He set them in place for ever and ever; he gave a decree that will never pass away.

READING
Bernard of Clairvaux

The name of Jesus is also nourishment. Haven't you felt stronger when you think of it? There is no other name that can similarly bless the one who meditates on it. It has the ability to refresh and strengthen. The best intellectual food is dry until it is dipped in this oil.

SPACE FOR REFLECTION

CLOSING PRAYERS
Lord, have mercy.
Christ, have mercy.
Lord, have mercy.

Our Father, who art in heaven. . . .

Lord, hear my prayer.
And let my cry come unto you.

COLLECT

God of all mercy and love, you are gracious, slow to anger, and abounding in steadfast love. Grant us grace to renounce evil and cling to Christ our Lord, that in every way we may prove to be your loving children. We ask this through the same Jesus Christ your Son, who lives and reigns with you and the Holy Spirit, one God forever and ever. Amen.

Lord, hear my prayer.
And let my cry come unto you.
Let us bless the Lord.
Thanks be to God.

May the souls of the faithful
by the mercy of God rest in peace.
Amen.
May divine help always be with us.
And with those who are absent from us.
Amen.

MIDDAY
SERVICE

Thursday
Week 2

O God, come to my assistance.
O Lord, make haste to help me.

OPENING PRAYER

Come, Creator Spirit, Paraclete, gift of God
most high, visit the souls of your people, and
fill with supernal grace the hearts which you
created. Amen.

PSALM 119:33–40

Teach me, O LORD, to follow your decrees;
then I will keep them to the end. Give me
understanding, and I will keep your law and
obey it with all my heart. Direct me in the
path of your commands, for there I find
delight. Turn my heart toward your statutes
and not toward selfish gain. Turn my eyes
away from worthless things; preserve my life
according to your word. Fulfill your promise
to your servant, so that you may be feared.
Take away the disgrace I dread, for your laws

are good. How I long for your precepts!
Preserve my life in your righteousness.

SPACE FOR REFLECTION

CLOSING PRAYERS
Let your mercy, O Lord, be upon us.
As we have hoped in you.

Lord, have mercy.
Christ, have mercy.
Lord, have mercy.

Our Father, who art in heaven. . . .

Lord, hear my prayer.
And let my cry come unto you.
Let us bless the Lord.
Thanks be to God.
May divine help always be with us.
And with those who are absent from us.
Amen.

VESPERS

Thursday
Week 2

O God, come to my assistance.
O Lord, make haste to help me.

OPENING PRAYER
O God of great power, you have rescued us
from error and from the weariness of death.
We give you thanks and praise. Amen.

PSALM 104:1–5, 10–15
Praise the LORD, O my soul. O LORD my
God, you are very great; you are clothed with
splendor and majesty. He wraps himself in
light as with a garment; he stretches out the
heavens like a tent and lays the beams of his
upper chambers on their waters. He makes
the clouds his chariot and rides on the wings
of the wind. He makes winds his messengers,
flames of fire his servants.

He set the earth on its foundations; it can
never be moved.

He makes springs pour water into the
ravines; it flows between the mountains.
They give water to all the beasts of the field;
the wild donkeys quench their thirst. The

birds of the air nest by the waters; they sing among the branches. He waters the mountains from his upper chambers; the earth is satisfied by the fruit of his work. He makes grass grow for the cattle, and plants for man to cultivate—bringing forth food from the earth: wine that gladdens the heart of man, oil to make his face shine, and bread that sustains his heart.

GOSPEL READING
John 8:31, 32
To the Jews who had believed him, Jesus said, "If you hold to my teaching, you are really my disciples. Then you will know the truth, and the truth will set you free."

SPACE FOR REFLECTION

CLOSING PRAYERS
Lord, have mercy.
Christ, have mercy.
Lord, have mercy.

Our Father, who art in heaven. . . .

Lord, hear my prayer.
And let my cry come unto you.

COLLECT

God of all mercy and love, you are gracious, slow to anger, and abounding in steadfast love. Grant us grace to renounce evil and cling to Christ our Lord, that in every way we may prove to be your loving children. We ask this through our Lord Jesus Christ your Son. Amen.

Lord, hear my prayer.
And let my cry come unto you.
Let us bless the Lord.
Thanks be to God.

May the souls of the faithful
by the mercy of God rest in peace.
Amen.
May divine help always be with us.
And with those who are absent from us.
Amen.

MORNING PRAYER

Friday
Week 2

O Lord, open my lips.
And my mouth will proclaim your praise.

OPENING PRAYER

O eternal Glory of heaven, blessed Hope of mortals, give your right hand to those who are getting up; let the soul arise sober and, ardent in praise, returning thanks to you. Amen.

PSALM 148:7–14

Praise the LORD from the earth, you great sea creatures and all ocean depths, lightning and hail, snow and clouds, stormy winds that do his bidding, you mountains and all hills, fruit trees and all cedars, wild animals and all cattle, small creatures and flying birds, kings of the earth and all nations, you princes and all rulers on earth, young men and maidens, old men and children.

Let them praise the name of the LORD, for his name alone is exalted; his splendor is above the earth and the heavens.

He has raised up for his people a horn, the praise of all his saints, of Israel, the people close to his heart. Praise the LORD.

READING
W. Paul Jones

Christians who permit themselves to be shaped by secular culture are guilty, not only of betraying God, but of losing their own true selves.

SPACE FOR REFLECTION

CLOSING PRAYERS
Lord, have mercy.
Christ, have mercy.
Lord, have mercy.

Our Father, who art in heaven. . . .

Lord, hear my prayer.
And let my cry come unto you.

COLLECT

Almighty God, ever-loving Father, your love was poured forth upon our world from the cross. As we have come to know the grace of our Lord's resurrection, grant that, through the power of your Spirit, we may rise with him to new life. We ask this through the same

Jesus Christ your Son, who lives and reigns with you and the Holy Spirit, one God forever and ever. Amen.

Lord, hear my prayer.
And let my cry come unto you.
Let us bless the Lord.
Thanks be to God.

May the souls of the faithful
by the mercy of God rest in peace.
Amen.
May divine help always be with us.
And with those who are absent from us.
Amen.

MIDDAY SERVICE

Friday
Week 2

O God, come to my assistance.
O Lord, make haste to help me.

OPENING PRAYER

Come, Holy Spirit, kindle light for our senses, pour out love in our hearts, and undergird with perpetual strength the weaknesses of our body. Amen.

PSALM 119:41–48

May your unfailing love come to me, O LORD, your salvation according to your promise; then I will answer the one who taunts me, for I trust in your word. Do not snatch the word of truth from my mouth, for I have put my hope in your laws. I will always obey your law, forever and ever. I will walk about in freedom, for I have sought out your precepts. I will speak of your statutes before kings and will not be put to shame, for I delight in your commands because I love

them. I lift up my hands to your commands,
which I love, and I meditate on your decrees.

SPACE FOR REFLECTION

CLOSING PRAYERS
Let your mercy, O Lord, be upon us.
As we have hoped in you.

Lord, have mercy.
Christ, have mercy.
Lord, have mercy.

Our Father, who art in heaven. . . .

Lord, hear my prayer.
And let my cry come unto you.
Let us bless the Lord.
Thanks be to God.
May divine help always be with us.
And with those who are absent from us.
Amen.

VESPERS

Friday
Week 2

O God, come to my assistance.
O Lord, make haste to help me.

OPENING PRAYER
O God, Maker of all mankind, give the rewards of joy, grant the gifts of graces, dissolve the chains of quarreling, and bind fast the agreements of peace. Amen.

PSALM 104:24–31
How many are your works, O LORD! In wisdom you made them all; the earth is full of your creatures. There is the sea, vast and spacious, teeming with creatures beyond number—living things both large and small. There the ships go to and fro, and the leviathan, which you formed to frolic there.

These all look to you to give them their food at the proper time. When you give it to them, they gather it up; when you open your hand, they are satisfied with good things. When you hide your face, they are terrified; when you take away their breath, they die and return to the dust. When you send your

Spirit, they are created, and you renew the face of the earth.

May the glory of the LORD endure forever; may the LORD rejoice in his works.

GOSPEL READING
John 8:34–36

Jesus replied, "I tell you the truth, everyone who sins is a slave to sin. Now a slave has no permanent place in the family, but a son belongs to it forever. So if the Son sets you free, you will be free indeed."

SPACE FOR REFLECTION

CLOSING PRAYERS
Lord, have mercy.
Christ, have mercy.
Lord, have mercy.

Our Father, who art in heaven. . . .

Lord, hear my prayer.
And let my cry come unto you.

COLLECT

Almighty God, ever-loving Father, your love was poured forth upon our world from the cross. As we have come to know the grace of our Lord's resurrection, grant that, through

the power of your Spirit, we may rise with
him to new life. We ask this through our
Lord Jesus Christ your Son. Amen.

Lord, hear my prayer.
And let my cry come unto you.
Let us bless the Lord.
Thanks be to God.

May the souls of the faithful
by the mercy of God rest in peace.
Amen.
May divine help always be with us.
And with those who are absent from us.
Amen.

MORNING PRAYER

Saturday
Week 2

O Lord, open my lips.
And my mouth will proclaim your praise.

OPENING PRAYER

O Light, shine on our senses and dispel the sleep of our soul. To you before all else may our voice resound, and let us pay our vows to you. Amen.

PSALM 149

Praise the LORD. Sing to the LORD a new song, his praise in the assembly of the saints.

Let Israel rejoice in their Maker; let the people of Zion be glad in their King. Let them praise his name with dancing and make music to him with tambourine and harp. For the LORD takes delight in his people; he crowns the humble with salvation. Let the saints rejoice in this honor and sing for joy on their beds. May the praise of God be in their mouths and a double-edged sword in their hands, to inflict vengeance on the nations and punishment on the peoples, to bind their kings with fetters, their nobles with shackles of iron, to carry out the sentence written against them. This is the glory of all his saints. Praise the LORD.

READING
Jeremy Taylor
Chastity is the duty which was mystically intended by God in the law of circumcision. It is the circumcision of the heart, the suppression of all irregular desires in the matter of sensual or carnal pleasure.

SPACE FOR REFLECTION

CLOSING PRAYERS
Lord, have mercy.
Christ, have mercy.
Lord, have mercy.

Our Father, who art in heaven. . . .

Lord, hear my prayer.
And let my cry come unto you.

COLLECT
Lord of the church, by your unfailing mercy you purify and guard your people. Since without you we cannot stand fast, support and guide us always by your grace. We ask

this through our Lord Jesus Christ your Son, who lives and reigns with you and the Holy Spirit, one God forever and ever. Amen.

Lord, hear my prayer.
And let my cry come unto you.
Let us bless the Lord.
Thanks be to God.

May the souls of the faithful
by the mercy of God rest in peace.
Amen.
May divine help always be with us.
And with those who are absent from us.
Amen.

MIDDAY SERVICE

Saturday
Week 2

O God, come to my assistance.
O Lord, make haste to help me.

OPENING PRAYER

Grant us a wholesome life, revive our zeal and love, O Father Almighty, through Jesus Christ the Lord, who reigns with you for all time with the Holy Spirit. Amen.

PSALM 119:49–56

Remember your word to your servant, for you have given me hope. My comfort in my suffering is this: Your promise preserves my life. The arrogant mock me without restraint, but I do not turn from your law. I remember your ancient laws, O LORD, and I find comfort in them. Indignation grips me because of the wicked, who have forsaken your law. Your decrees are the theme of my song wherever I lodge. In the night I remember your name, O LORD, and I will keep your law. This has been my practice: I obey your precepts.

SPACE FOR REFLECTION

CLOSING PRAYERS
Let your mercy, O Lord, be upon us.
As we have hoped in you.

Lord, have mercy.
Christ, have mercy.
Lord, have mercy.

Our Father, who art in heaven. . . .

Lord, hear my prayer.
And let my cry come unto you.
Let us bless the Lord.
Thanks be to God.
May divine help always be with us.
And with those who are absent from us.
Amen.

VESPERS

Saturday
Week 2

O God, come to my assistance.
O Lord, make haste to help me.

OPENING PRAYER

O God, Creator of all things and Ruler of heaven, we give thanks for the day that is finished and we pray at the start of the night. May faith not know darkness; may the night shine with faith. Amen.

PSALM 138

I will praise you, O LORD, with all my heart; before the "gods" I will sing your praise. I will bow down toward your holy temple and will praise your name for your love and your faithfulness, for you have exalted above all things your name and your word. When I called, you answered me; you made me bold and stouthearted.

May all the kings of the earth praise you, O LORD, when they hear the words of your mouth. May they sing of the ways of the LORD, for the glory of the LORD is great.

Though the LORD is on high, he looks upon the lowly, but the proud he knows from afar. Though I walk in the midst of trouble, you preserve my life; you stretch out your hand against the anger of my foes, with your right hand you save me. The LORD will fulfill his purpose for me; your love, O LORD, endures forever—do not abandon the works of your hands.

GOSPEL READING
John 9:24, 25

A second time they summoned the man who had been blind. "Give glory to God," they said. "We know this man is a sinner."

He replied, "Whether he is a sinner or not, I don't know. One thing I do know. I was blind but now I see."

SILENT MEDITATION

CLOSING PRAYERS
Lord, have mercy.
Christ, have mercy.
Lord, have mercy.

Our Father, who art in heaven. . . .

Lord, hear my prayer.
And let my cry come unto you.

COLLECT

Lord of the church, by your unfailing mercy you purify and guard your people. Since without you we cannot stand fast, support and guide us always by your grace. We pray this in the name of our Lord and Savior Jesus Christ. Amen.

Lord, hear my prayer.
And let my cry come unto you.
Let us bless the Lord.
Thanks be to God.

May the souls of the faithful
by the mercy of God rest in peace.
Amen.
May divine help always be with us.
And with those who are absent from us.
Amen.

WEEK 3

MORNING PRAYER

Sunday
Week 3

O Lord, open my lips.
And my mouth will proclaim your praise.

OPENING PRAYER

May our compassionate God drive away all our anguish, bestow health, and give us by the loving-kindness of the Father, the kingdom of the heavens. Amen.

PSALM 63:1–8

O God, you are my God, earnestly I seek you; my soul thirsts for you, my body longs for you, in a dry and weary land where there is no water.

I have seen you in the sanctuary and beheld your power and your glory. Because your love is better than life, my lips will glorify you. I will praise you as long as I live, and in your name I will lift up my hands. My soul will be satisfied as with the richest of foods; with singing lips my mouth will praise you.

On my bed I remember you; I think of you through the watches of the night. Because you are my help, I sing in the shadow of your wings. My soul clings to you; your right hand upholds me.

READING
Brother Lawrence of the Resurrection
We must not grow weary of doing little things for the love of God, who looks not on the great size of the work, but on the love in it.

SPACE FOR REFLECTION

BENEDICTUS
Canticle of Zechariah: Luke 1:68–79
"Praise be to the Lord, the God of Israel, because he has come and has redeemed his people. He has raised up a horn of salvation for us in the house of his servant David (as he said through his holy prophets of long ago), salvation from our enemies and from the hand of all who hate us—to show mercy to our fathers and to remember his holy covenant, the oath he swore to our father Abraham: to rescue us from the hand of our enemies, and to enable us to serve him without fear in holiness and righteousness before him all our days.

And you, my child, will be called a prophet of the Most High; for you will go on before the Lord to prepare the way for him, to give his people the knowledge of salvation through the forgiveness of their sins, because of the tender mercy of our God, by which the rising sun will come to us from heaven to shine on those living in darkness and in the shadow of death, to guide our feet into the path of peace."

CLOSING PRAYERS

Lord, have mercy.
Christ, have mercy.
Lord, have mercy.

Our Father, who art in heaven. . . .

Lord, hear my prayer.
And let my cry come unto you.

COLLECT

Eternal Lord our God, the beginning and end of our lives, give us grace to serve you with joy, that we might know that our full and lasting happiness is a life of constant service to you and our neighbor. We ask this through our Lord Jesus Christ your Son, who lives and reigns with you and the Holy Spirit, one God forever and ever. Amen.

Lord, hear my prayer.
And let my cry come unto you.
Let us bless the Lord.
Thanks be to God.

May the souls of the faithful
by the mercy of God rest in peace.
Amen.
May divine help always be with us.
And with those who are absent from us.
Amen.

MIDDAY SERVICE

Sunday
Week 3

O God, come to my assistance.
O Lord, make haste to help me.

OPENING PRAYER

Mighty Ruler, true God, you who regulate the functions of all things and provide the morning its splendor, the midday its heat. Extinguish the flames of quarrels, take away harmful passions, grant healing of body and true peace of heart. Amen.

PSALM 119:57–64

You are my portion, O LORD; I have promised to obey your words. I have sought your face with all my heart; be gracious to me according to your promise. I have considered my ways and have turned my steps to your statutes. I will hasten and not delay to obey your commands. Though the wicked bind me with ropes, I will not forget your law. At midnight I rise to give you thanks for your righteous laws. I am a friend to all who fear

127

you, to all who follow your precepts. The earth is filled with your love, O LORD; teach me your decrees.

SPACE FOR REFLECTION

CLOSING PRAYERS
Let your mercy, O Lord, be upon us.
As we have hoped in you.

Lord, have mercy.
Christ, have mercy.
Lord, have mercy.

Our Father, who art in heaven. . . .

Lord, hear my prayer.
And let my cry come unto you.
Let us bless the Lord.
Thanks be to God.
May divine help always be with us.
And with those who are absent from us.
Amen.

VESPERS

Sunday
Week 3

O God, come to my assistance.
O Lord, make haste to help me.

OPENING PRAYER
O Light, blessed Trinity and perfect Unity, already the fiery sun is receding; pour the light of your presence into our hearts. Amen.

PSALM 113
Praise the LORD. Praise, O servants of the LORD, praise the name of the LORD. Let the name of the LORD be praised, both now and forevermore. From the rising of the sun to the place where it sets, the name of the LORD is to be praised. The LORD is exalted over all the nations, his glory above the heavens. Who is like the LORD our God, the One who sits enthroned on high, who stoops down to look on the heavens and the earth?

He raises the poor from the dust and lifts the needy from the ash heap; he seats them with princes, with the princes of their people. He settles the barren woman in her home as a happy mother of children. Praise the LORD.

GOSPEL READING
John 10:14–16

"I am the good shepherd; I know my sheep and my sheep know me—just as the Father knows me and I know the Father—and I lay down my life for the sheep. I have other sheep that are not of this sheep pen. I must bring them also. They too will listen to my voice, and there shall be one flock and one shepherd."

SPACE FOR REFLECTION

MAGNIFICAT
The Canticle of Mary: Luke 1:46b–55

"My soul glorifies the Lord and my spirit rejoices in God my Savior, for he has been mindful of the humble state of his servant. From now on all generations will call me blessed, for the Mighty One has done great things for me—holy is his name. His mercy extends to those who fear him, from generation to generation. He has performed mighty deeds with his arm; he has scattered those who are proud in their inmost thoughts. He has brought down rulers from their thrones but has lifted up the humble. He has filled the hungry with good things but has sent the rich away empty. He has helped his servant

Israel, remembering to be merciful to Abraham and his descendants forever, even as he said to our fathers."

CLOSING PRAYERS
Lord, have mercy.
Christ, have mercy.
Lord, have mercy.

Our Father, who art in heaven. . . .

Lord, hear my prayer.
And let my cry come unto you.

COLLECT
Eternal Lord our God, the beginning and end of our lives, give us grace to serve you with joy, that we might know that our full and lasting happiness is a life of constant service to you and our neighbor. We ask this through our Lord Jesus Christ your Son, who lives and reigns with you and the Holy Spirit, one God forever and ever. Amen.

Lord, hear my prayer.
And let my cry come unto you.
Let us bless the Lord.
Thanks be to God.

May the souls of the faithful
by the mercy of God rest in peace.
Amen.
May divine help always be with us.
And with those who are absent from us.
Amen.

MORNING PRAYER

Monday
Week 3

O Lord, open my lips.
And my mouth will proclaim your praise.

OPENING PRAYER

Lord Jesus, Splendor of the Father's glory, O true Sun, descend, sparkling with uninterrupted brightness; O radiance of the Holy Spirit, pour in upon our senses. Amen.

PSALM 61

Hear my cry, O God; listen to my prayer. From the ends of the earth I call to you, I call as my heart grows faint; lead me to the rock that is higher than I. For you have been my refuge, a strong tower against the foe.

I long to dwell in your tent forever and take refuge in the shelter of your wings.

For you have heard my vows, O God; you have given me the heritage of those who fear your name.

Increase the days of the king's life, his years for many generations. May he be

enthroned in God's presence forever; appoint
your love and faithfulness to protect him.

Then will I ever sing praise to your name
and fulfill my vows day after day.

READING
Daniel Homan, O.S.B., and Lonni Collins Pratt
It is a great loss if we greet every day with
clenched hands stuffed with our own devices.
We will never know what is out there waiting
for us if we don't extend an empty hand to
the world and wait for the wonder to happen.

SPACE FOR REFLECTION

CLOSING PRAYERS
Lord, have mercy.
Christ, have mercy.
Lord, have mercy.

Our Father, who art in heaven. . . .

Lord, hear my prayer.
And let my cry come unto you.

COLLECT

Almighty, eternal God, every good gift comes from you. Increase our faith, fill our hearts with love for you, and guide us through this life until we inherit life eternal. We ask this through our Lord Jesus Christ your Son. Amen.

Lord, hear my prayer.
And let my cry come unto you.
Let us bless the Lord.
Thanks be to God.

May the souls of the faithful
by the mercy of God rest in peace.
Amen.
May divine help always be with us.
And with those who are absent from us.
Amen.

MIDDAY SERVICE

Monday
Week 3

O God, come to my assistance.
O Lord, make haste to help me.

OPENING PRAYER

O Christ, you are the Light, the Splendor of the Father, and the eternal Hope of all things. Listen to the prayers which your servants throughout the world pour forth. Amen.

PSALM 119:65–72

Do good to your servant according to your word, O LORD. Teach me knowledge and good judgment, for I believe in your commands. Before I was afflicted I went astray, but now I obey your word. You are good, and what you do is good; teach me your decrees. Though the arrogant have smeared me with lies, I keep your precepts with all my heart. Their hearts are callous and unfeeling, but I delight in your law. It was good for me to be afflicted so that I might learn your decrees. The law from your mouth is more precious to me than thousands of pieces of silver and gold.

SPACE FOR REFLECTION

CLOSING PRAYERS
Let your mercy, O Lord, be upon us.
As we have hoped in you.

Lord, have mercy.
Christ, have mercy.
Lord, have mercy.

Our Father, who art in heaven. . . .

Lord, hear my prayer.
And let my cry come unto you.
Let us bless the Lord.
Thanks be to God.
May divine help always be with us.
And with those who are absent from us.
Amen.

VESPERS

Monday
Week 3

O God, come to my assistance.
O Lord, make haste to help me.

OPENING PRAYER

Pour into us now, O most loving One, the gift of eternal grace, so that, by the misfortunes of new deception, old error may not destroy us. Amen.

PSALM 89:1, 2, 5–8

I will sing of the LORD's great love forever; with my mouth I will make your faithfulness known through all generations. I will declare that your love stands firm forever, that you established your faithfulness in heaven itself.

The heavens praise your wonders, O LORD, your faithfulness too, in the assembly of the holy ones. For who in the skies above can compare with the LORD? Who is like the LORD among the heavenly beings? In the council of the holy ones God is greatly feared; he is more awesome than all who surround him. O LORD God Almighty, who is like you?

You are mighty, O LORD, and your faithfulness surrounds you.

GOSPEL READING
John 11:17, 20–22

On his arrival, Jesus found that Lazarus had already been in the tomb for four days. When Martha heard that Jesus was coming, she went out to meet him, but Mary stayed at home.

"Lord," Martha said to Jesus, "if you had been here, my brother would not have died. But I know that even now God will give you whatever you ask."

SPACE FOR REFLECTION

CLOSING PRAYERS
Lord, have mercy.
Christ, have mercy.
Lord, have mercy.

Our Father, who art in heaven. . . .

Lord, hear my prayer.
And let my cry come unto you.

COLLECT

Almighty, eternal God, every good gift comes from you. Increase our faith, fill our hearts with love for you, and guide us through this life until we inherit life eternal. We ask this through our Lord Jesus Christ your Son, who lives and reigns with you and the Holy Spirit, one God forever and ever. Amen.

Lord, hear my prayer.
And let my cry come unto you.
Let us bless the Lord.
Thanks be to God.

May the souls of the faithful
by the mercy of God rest in peace.
Amen.
May divine help always be with us.
And with those who are absent from us.
Amen.

MORNING PRAYER

Tuesday
Week 3

O Lord, open my lips.
And my mouth will proclaim your praise.

OPENING PRAYER

O Christ, dispel sleep, break the chains of night, release long-standing sin, and pour in new light. Amen.

PSALM 66:1–4, 8, 9, 16–20

Shout with joy to God, all the earth! Sing the glory of his name; make his praise glorious! Say to God, "How awesome are your deeds! So great is your power that your enemies cringe before you. All the earth bows down to you; they sing praise to you, they sing praise to your name."

Praise our God, O peoples, let the sound of his praise be heard; he has preserved our lives and kept our feet from slipping.

Come and listen, all you who fear God; let me tell you what he has done for me. I cried out to him with my mouth; his praise was on my tongue. If I had cherished sin in my heart, the Lord would not have listened; but God has surely listened and heard my voice in prayer. Praise be to God, who has not rejected my prayer or withheld his love from me!

READING
Jean-Pierre de Caussade

A heart that has no other wish but to possess God must attract him to itself, and this secret of love is a very great one, since by this way alone sure faith and firm hope are established in the soul. Then it is that we believe what we cannot see, and expect to possess what we cannot feel.

SPACE FOR REFLECTION

CLOSING PRAYERS
Lord, have mercy.
Christ, have mercy.
Lord, have mercy.

Our Father, who art in heaven. . . .

Lord, hear my prayer.
And let my cry come unto you.

COLLECT

O God, the Father of all humankind, you bid us listen to your Son, the well-beloved. Nourish our hearts on your word, purify the eyes of our mind, and fill us with joy at the vision of your glory. We ask this through our Lord Jesus Christ your Son, who lives and reigns with you and the Holy Spirit, one God forever and ever. Amen.

Lord, hear my prayer.
And let my cry come unto you.
Let us bless the Lord.
Thanks be to God.

May the souls of the faithful
by the mercy of God rest in peace.
Amen.
May divine help always be with us.
And with those who are absent from us.
Amen.

MIDDAY SERVICE

Tuesday
Week 3

O God, come to my assistance.
O Lord, make haste to help me.

OPENING PRAYER

O Jesus, our redemption, love, and desire,
may your love constrain you to pass over our
evils, sparing us, and having answered our
prayer, may you satisfy us with your face.
Amen.

PSALM 119:73–80

Your hands made me and formed me; give
me understanding to learn your commands.
May those who fear you rejoice when they see
me, for I have put my hope in your word. I
know, O LORD, that your laws are righteous,
and in faithfulness you have afflicted me.
May your unfailing love be my comfort,
according to your promise to your servant.
Let your compassion come to me that I may
live, for your law is my delight. May the
arrogant be put to shame for wronging me

without cause; but I will meditate on your precepts. May those who fear you turn to me, those who understand your statutes. May my heart be blameless toward your decrees, that I may not be put to shame.

SPACE FOR REFLECTION

CLOSING PRAYERS
Let your mercy, O Lord, be upon us.
As we have hoped in you.

Lord, have mercy.
Christ, have mercy.
Lord, have mercy.

Our Father, who art in heaven. . . .

Lord, hear my prayer.
And let my cry come unto you.
Let us bless the Lord.
Thanks be to God.

May divine help always be with us.
And with those who are absent from us.
Amen.

VESPERS

Tuesday
Week 3

O God, come to my assistance.
O Lord, make haste to help me.

OPENING PRAYER

O great Creator of the earth, cleanse the wounds of our souls with the freshness of your grace, destroy wrong impulses, and let us be filled with your good things. Amen.

PSALM 127

Unless the LORD builds the house, its builders labor in vain. Unless the LORD watches over the city, the watchmen stand guard in vain. In vain you rise early and stay up late, toiling for food to eat—for he grants sleep to those he loves.

Sons are a heritage from the LORD, children a reward from him. Like arrows in the hands of a warrior are sons born in one's youth. Blessed is the man whose quiver is full of them. They will not be put to shame when they contend with their enemies in the gate.

GOSPEL READING
John 11:23–27

Jesus said to her, "Your brother will rise again."

Martha answered, "I know he will rise again at the resurrection at the last day."

Jesus said to her, "I am the resurrection and the life. He who believes in me will live, even though he dies; and whoever lives and believes in me will never die. Do you believe this?"

"Yes, Lord," she told him, "I believe that you are the Christ, the Son of God, who was to come into the world."

SPACE FOR REFLECTION

CLOSING PRAYERS
Lord, have mercy.
Christ, have mercy.
Lord, have mercy.

Our Father, who art in heaven. . . .

Lord, hear my prayer.
And let my cry come unto you.

COLLECT
O God, the Father of all humankind, you bid us listen to your Son, the well-beloved.

Nourish our hearts on your word, purify the eyes of our mind, and fill us with joy at the vision of your glory. We pray this in the name of our Lord and Savior Jesus Christ. Amen.

Lord, hear my prayer.
And let my cry come unto you.
Let us bless the Lord.
Thanks be to God.

May the souls of the faithful
by the mercy of God rest in peace.
Amen.
May divine help always be with us.
And with those who are absent from us.
Amen.

MORNING PRAYER

Wednesday
Week 3

O Lord, open my lips.
And my mouth will proclaim your praise.

OPENING PRAYER
To you, O Christ, King most loving, and to the Father be glory with the Spirit, the Paraclete, for everlasting ages. Amen.

PSALM 72:1–9, 17–19
Endow the king with your justice, O God, the royal son with your righteousness. He will judge your people in righteousness, your afflicted ones with justice. The mountains will bring prosperity to the people, the hills the fruit of righteousness. He will defend the afflicted among the people and save the children of the needy; he will crush the oppressor.

He will endure as long as the sun, as long as the moon, through all generations. He will be like rain falling on a mown field, like showers watering the earth. In his days the righteous will flourish; prosperity will abound till the moon is no more.

May his name endure forever; may it continue as long as the sun.

All nations will be blessed through him, and they will call him blessed. Praise be to the Lord God, the God of Israel, who alone does marvelous deeds. Praise be to his glorious name forever; may the whole earth be filled with his glory. Amen and Amen.

READING
Robert Waldron

The flickering red vigil lamp on the altar whispered the presence of Christ in the tabernacle. If truly present, I thought, Jesus would be aware of me, looking directly at me. What would he say to me sitting here alone in a choir stall? What would I say? Perhaps there'd be nothing to say. Perhaps silence would be enough.

SPACE FOR REFLECTION

CLOSING PRAYERS
Lord, have mercy.
Christ, have mercy.
Lord, have mercy.

Our Father, who art in heaven. . . .

Lord, hear my prayer.
And let my cry come unto you.

COLLECT
Most merciful and loving God, your blessed
Son suffered and died for us. Grant us grace
to endure the sufferings of this present time,
to overcome all that seeks to overwhelm us,
and to be confident of the glory that shall be
revealed in us. We ask this through our Lord
Jesus Christ your Son, who lives and reigns
with you and the Holy Spirit, one God forever
and ever. Amen.

Lord, hear my prayer.
And let my cry come unto you.
Let us bless the Lord.
Thanks be to God.

May the souls of the faithful
by the mercy of God rest in peace.
Amen.
May divine help always be with us.
And with those who are absent from us.
Amen.

MIDDAY
SERVICE

Wednesday
Week 3

O God, come to my assistance.
O Lord, make haste to help me.

OPENING PRAYER
Jesus, Lord God and Creator of all things, be
yourself our joy, you who are the future prize.
May our glory be in you always, through all
the ages. Amen.

PSALM 119:81–88
My soul faints with longing for your salvation,
but I have put my hope in your word. My
eyes fail, looking for your promise; I say,
"When will you comfort me?" Though I am
like a wineskin in the smoke, I do not forget
your decrees. How long must your servant
wait? When will you punish my persecutors?
The arrogant dig pitfalls for me, contrary to
your law. All your commands are trustworthy;
help me, for men persecute me without
cause. They almost wiped me from the earth,
but I have not forsaken your precepts.

Preserve my life according to your love, and I will obey the statutes of your mouth.

SPACE FOR REFLECTION

CLOSING PRAYERS
Let your mercy, O Lord, be upon us.
As we have hoped in you.

Lord, have mercy.
Christ, have mercy.
Lord, have mercy.

Our Father, who art in heaven. . . .

Lord, hear my prayer.
And let my cry come unto you.
Let us bless the Lord.
Thanks be to God.
May divine help always be with us.
And with those who are absent from us.
Amen.

VESPERS

Wednesday
Week 3

O God, come to my assistance.
O Lord, make haste to help me.

OPENING PRAYER

Most holy God of heaven, you who paint the shining center of the sky with the brightness of fire, illumine our hearts, banish sordid things, release the chain of guilt, and make void our crimes. Amen.

PSALM 103:1–5, 8–14

Praise the LORD, O my soul; all my inmost being, praise his holy name. Praise the LORD, O my soul, and forget not all his benefits— who forgives all your sins and heals all your diseases, who redeems your life from the pit and crowns you with love and compassion, who satisfies your desires with good things so that your youth is renewed like the eagle's.

The LORD is compassionate and gracious, slow to anger, abounding in love. He will not always accuse, nor will he harbor his anger forever; he does not treat us as our sins deserve or repay us according to our iniquities. For as high as the heavens are above the earth, so great is his love for those who fear him; as far as the east is from the west, so far has he removed our transgressions from us. As a father has compassion on his children, so the LORD has compassion on those who fear him; for he knows how we are formed, he remembers that we are dust.

GOSPEL READING
John 11:32–35

When Mary reached the place where Jesus was and saw him, she fell at his feet and said, "Lord, if you had been here, my brother would not have died."

When Jesus saw her weeping, and the Jews who had come along with her also weeping, he was deeply moved in spirit and troubled. "Where have you laid him?" he asked. "Come and see, Lord," they replied. Jesus wept.

SPACE FOR REFLECTION

CLOSING PRAYERS
Lord, have mercy.
Christ, have mercy.
Lord, have mercy.

Our Father, who art in heaven. . . .

Lord, hear my prayer.
And let my cry come unto you.

COLLECT

Most merciful and loving God, your blessed Son suffered and died for us. Grant us grace to endure the sufferings of this present time, to overcome all that seeks to overwhelm us, and to be confident of the glory that shall be revealed in us. We ask this through our Lord Jesus Christ your Son. Amen.

Lord, hear my prayer.
And let my cry come unto you.
Let us bless the Lord.
Thanks be to God.

May the souls of the faithful
by the mercy of God rest in peace.
Amen.
May divine help always be with us.
And with those who are absent from us.
Amen.

MORNING PRAYER

Thursday
Week 3

O Lord, open my lips.
And my mouth will proclaim your praise.

OPENING PRAYER

Behold, the fiery sun is rising; may blindness at last depart—let us speak nothing underhanded, let us consider nothing dark. To God the Father be glory, and to his only Son, with the Spirit, the Paraclete, for everlasting ages. Amen.

PSALM 86:1–7, 11–13

Hear, O LORD, and answer me, for I am poor and needy. Guard my life, for I am devoted to you. You are my God; save your servant who trusts in you. Have mercy on me, O Lord, for I call to you all day long. Bring joy to your servant, for to you, O Lord, I lift up my soul.

You are forgiving and good, O Lord, abounding in love to all who call to you. Hear my prayer, O LORD; listen to my cry for mercy. In the day of my trouble I will call to you, for you will answer me. Teach me your way, O LORD, and I will walk in your truth; give me an undivided heart, that I may fear your name. I will praise you, O LORD my God, with all my heart; I will glorify your name forever. For great is your love toward me; you have delivered me from the depths of the grave.

READING
Teresa of Avila

We must be firmly convinced that if we fight courageously and do not allow ourselves to be beaten, we will get what we want. No matter how small our gains, they will make us very rich. Do not be afraid that the Lord who has called us to drink of this spring will allow us to die of thirst.

SPACE FOR REFLECTION

CLOSING PRAYERS
Lord, have mercy.
Christ, have mercy.
Lord, have mercy.

Our Father, who art in heaven. . . .

Lord, hear my prayer.
And let my cry come unto you.

COLLECT

O loving heavenly Father, whose blessed Son did suffer for the whole world, grant that we may know you better, love you more, and serve you with a more perfect will. We ask this through our Lord Jesus Christ your Son, who lives and reigns with you and the Holy Spirit, one God forever and ever. Amen.

Lord, hear my prayer.
And let my cry come unto you.
Let us bless the Lord.
Thanks be to God.

May the souls of the faithful
by the mercy of God rest in peace.
Amen.
May divine help always be with us.
And with those who are absent from us.
Amen.

MIDDAY SERVICE

Thursday
Week 3

O God, come to my assistance.
O Lord, make haste to help me.

OPENING PRAYER
Come, Creator Spirit, Paraclete, gift of God most high, visit the souls of your people, and fill with supernal grace the hearts which you created. Amen.

PSALM 119:89–96
Your word, O LORD, is eternal; it stands firm in the heavens. Your faithfulness continues through all generations; you established the earth, and it endures. Your laws endure to this day, for all things serve you. If your law had not been my delight, I would have perished in my affliction. I will never forget your precepts, for by them you have preserved my life. Save me, for I am yours; I have sought out your precepts. The wicked are waiting to destroy me, but I will ponder your statutes. To all perfection I see a limit; but your commands are boundless.

SPACE FOR REFLECTION

CLOSING PRAYERS

Let your mercy, O Lord, be upon us.
As we have hoped in you.

Lord, have mercy.
Christ, have mercy.
Lord, have mercy.

Our Father, who art in heaven. . . .

Lord, hear my prayer.
And let my cry come unto you.
Let us bless the Lord.
Thanks be to God.
May divine help always be with us.
And with those who are absent from us.
Amen.

VESPERS

Thursday
Week 3

O God, come to my assistance.
O Lord, make haste to help me.

OPENING PRAYER

O God of great power, you have rescued us from error and from the weariness of death. We give you thanks and praise. Amen.

PSALM 130

Out of the depths I cry to you, O LORD; O Lord, hear my voice. Let your ears be attentive to my cry for mercy.

If you, O LORD, kept a record of sins, O Lord, who could stand? But with you there is forgiveness; therefore you are feared.

I wait for the LORD, my soul waits, and in his word I put my hope. My soul waits for the Lord more than watchmen wait for the morning, more than watchmen wait for the morning.

O Israel, put your hope in the LORD, for with the LORD is unfailing love and with him is full redemption. He himself will redeem Israel from all their sins.

GOSPEL READING
John 11:41–44

So they took away the stone. Then Jesus looked up and said, "Father, I thank you that you have heard me. I knew that you always hear me, but I said this for the benefit of the people standing here, that they may believe that you sent me."

When he had said this, Jesus called in a loud voice, "Lazarus, come out!" The dead man came out, his hands and feet wrapped with strips of linen, and a cloth around his face.

SPACE FOR REFLECTION

CLOSING PRAYERS
Lord, have mercy.
Christ, have mercy.
Lord, have mercy.

Our Father, who art in heaven. . . .

Lord, hear my prayer.
And let my cry come unto you.

COLLECT
O loving heavenly Father, whose blessed Son did suffer for the whole world, grant that we

may know you better, love you more, and serve you with a more perfect will. We ask this through our Lord Jesus Christ your Son, who lives and reigns with you and the Holy Spirit, one God forever and ever. Amen.

Lord, hear my prayer.
And let my cry come unto you.
Let us bless the Lord.
Thanks be to God.

May the souls of the faithful
by the mercy of God rest in peace.
Amen.
May divine help always be with us.
And with those who are absent from us.
Amen.

MORNING PRAYER

Friday
Week 3

O Lord, open my lips.
And my mouth will proclaim your praise.

OPENING PRAYER

O eternal Glory of heaven, blessed Hope of mortals, give your right hand to those who are getting up; let the soul arise sober and, ardent in praise, returning thanks to you. Amen.

PSALM 85:1–9

You showed favor to your land, O LORD; you restored the fortunes of Jacob. You forgave the iniquity of your people and covered all their sins.

You set aside all your wrath and turned from your fierce anger.

Restore us again, O God our Savior, and put away your displeasure toward us. Will you be angry with us forever? Will you prolong your anger through all generations? Will you not revive us again, that your people may rejoice in you? Show us your unfailing love, O LORD, and grant us your salvation.

I will listen to what God the LORD will say; he promises peace to his people, his saints—but let them not return to folly. Surely his salvation is near those who fear him, that his glory may dwell in our land.

READING
M. Basil Pennington, O.C.S.O.
If we realized and were constantly conscious that whatever we do to each other, to any human person, we do to Jesus, to the Son of God, to our beloved Savior, how then would we act?

SPACE FOR REFLECTION

CLOSING PRAYERS
Lord, have mercy.
Christ, have mercy.
Lord, have mercy.

Our Father, who art in heaven. . . .

Lord, hear my prayer.
And let my cry come unto you.

COLLECT

Gracious and eternal Lord, in your bounty you have sent us your Holy Spirit. May he teach us to think and do what is right, so that we, who without you cannot exist, may live in loving obedience to your will. We ask this through our Lord Jesus Christ your Son, who lives and reigns with you and the Holy Spirit, one God forever and ever. Amen.

Lord, hear my prayer.
And let my cry come unto you.
Let us bless the Lord.
Thanks be to God.

May the souls of the faithful
by the mercy of God rest in peace.
Amen.
May divine help always be with us.
And with those who are absent from us.
Amen.

MIDDAY SERVICE

Friday
Week 3

O God, come to my assistance.
O Lord, make haste to help me.

OPENING PRAYER

Come, Holy Spirit, kindle light for our senses, pour out love in our hearts, and undergird with perpetual strength the weaknesses of our body. Amen.

PSALM 119:97–104

Oh, how I love your law! I meditate on it all day long. Your commands make me wiser than my enemies, for they are ever with me. I have more insight than all my teachers, for I meditate on your statutes. I have more understanding than the elders, for I obey your precepts. I have kept my feet from every evil path so that I might obey your word. I have not departed from your laws, for you yourself have taught me. How sweet are your words to my taste, sweeter than honey to my mouth! I gain understanding from your precepts; therefore I hate every wrong path.

SPACE FOR REFLECTION

CLOSING PRAYERS

Let your mercy, O Lord, be upon us.
As we have hoped in you.

Lord, have mercy.
Christ, have mercy.
Lord, have mercy.

Our Father, who art in heaven. . . .

Lord, hear my prayer.
And let my cry come unto you.
Let us bless the Lord.
Thanks be to God.
May divine help always be with us.
And with those who are absent from us.
Amen.

VESPERS

Friday
Week 3

O God, come to my assistance.
O Lord, make haste to help me.

OPENING PRAYER

O God, Maker of all mankind, give the
rewards of joy, grant the gifts of graces, dissolve
the chains of quarreling, and bind fast the
agreements of peace. Amen.

PSALM 90:1–6, 12–14

Lord, you have been our dwelling place
throughout all generations. Before the
mountains were born or you brought forth
the earth and the world, from everlasting to
everlasting you are God.

You turn men back to dust, saying,
"Return to dust, O sons of men." For a
thousand years in your sight are like a day
that has just gone by, or like a watch in the
night. You sweep men away in the sleep of
death; they are like the new grass of the
morning though in the morning it springs
up new, by evening it is dry and withered.

Teach us to number our days aright, that we may gain a heart of wisdom. Relent, O Lord! How long will it be? Have compassion on your servants. Satisfy us in the morning with your unfailing love, that we may sing for joy and be glad all our days.

GOSPEL READING
John 12:23–25

Jesus replied, "The hour has come for the Son of Man to be glorified. I tell you the truth, unless a kernel of wheat falls to the ground and dies, it remains only a single seed. But if it dies, it produces many seeds. The man who loves his life will lose it, while the man who hates his life in this world will keep it for eternal life."

SPACE FOR REFLECTION

CLOSING PRAYERS

Lord, have mercy.
Christ, have mercy.
Lord, have mercy.

Our Father, who art in heaven. . . .

Lord, hear my prayer.
And let my cry come unto you.

COLLECT

Gracious and eternal Lord, in your bounty you have sent us your Holy Spirit. May he teach us to think and do what is right, so that we, who without you cannot exist, may live in loving obedience to your will. We ask this through our Lord Jesus Christ your Son. Amen.

Lord, hear my prayer.
And let my cry come unto you.
Let us bless the Lord.
Thanks be to God.

May the souls of the faithful
by the mercy of God rest in peace.
Amen.
May divine help always be with us.
And with those who are absent from us.
Amen.

MORNING PRAYER

Saturday
Week 3

O Lord, open my lips.
And my mouth will proclaim your praise.

OPENING PRAYER

O Light, shine on our senses and dispel the sleep of our soul. To you before all else may our voice resound, and let us pay our vows to you. Amen.

PSALM 84:1, 2, 4, 10–12

How lovely is your dwelling place, O LORD Almighty! My soul yearns, even faints, for the courts of the LORD; my heart and my flesh cry out for the living God. . . . Blessed are those who dwell in your house; they are ever praising you.

Better is one day in your courts than a thousand elsewhere; I would rather be a doorkeeper in the house of my God than dwell in the tents of the wicked. For the LORD God is a sun and shield; the LORD bestows favor and honor; no good thing does he withhold from those whose walk is blameless.

O Lord Almighty, blessed is the man who trusts in you.

READING
Jeremy Taylor

God is specially present in the hearts of his people by his Holy Spirit. Indeed the hearts of holy men are truly his temples. In type and foreshadow, they are heaven itself. For God reigns in the hearts of his servants. There is his kingdom.

SPACE FOR REFLECTION

CLOSING PRAYERS
Lord, have mercy.
Christ, have mercy.
Lord, have mercy.

Our Father, who art in heaven. . . .

Lord, hear my prayer.
And let my cry come unto you.

COLLECT

Almighty God our heavenly Father, whose grace here on earth brings us the gifts of heaven, guide us in this present life, and so lead us now, that we might dwell in the light of your eternal love. We ask this through our Lord Jesus Christ your Son, who lives and reigns with you and the Holy Spirit, one God forever and ever. Amen.

Lord, hear my prayer.
And let my cry come unto you.
Let us bless the Lord.
Thanks be to God.

May the souls of the faithful
by the mercy of God rest in peace.
Amen.
May divine help always be with us.
And with those who are absent from us.
Amen.

MIDDAY SERVICE

Saturday
Week 3

O God, come to my assistance.
O Lord, make haste to help me.

OPENING PRAYER

Grant us a wholesome life, revive our zeal and love, O Father Almighty, through Jesus Christ the Lord, who reigns with you for all time with the Holy Spirit. Amen.

PSALM 119:105–112

Your word is a lamp to my feet and a light for my path. I have taken an oath and confirmed it, that I will follow your righteous laws. I have suffered much; preserve my life, O LORD, according to your word. Accept, O LORD, the willing praise of my mouth, and teach me your laws. Though I constantly take my life in my hands, I will not forget your law. The wicked have set a snare for me, but I have not strayed from your precepts. Your statutes are my heritage forever; they are the joy of my heart. My heart is set on keeping your decrees to the very end.

SPACE FOR REFLECTION

CLOSING PRAYERS

Let your mercy, O Lord, be upon us.
As we have hoped in you.

Lord, have mercy.
Christ, have mercy.
Lord, have mercy.

Our Father, who art in heaven. . . .

Lord, hear my prayer.
And let my cry come unto you.
Let us bless the Lord.
Thanks be to God.
May divine help always be with us.
And with those who are absent from us.
Amen.

VESPERS

Saturday
Week 3

O God, come to my assistance.
O Lord, make haste to help me.

OPENING PRAYER

O God, Creator of all things and Ruler of heaven, we give thanks for the day that is finished and we pray at the start of the night. May faith not know darkness; may the night shine with faith. Amen.

PSALM 71:1–6, 17, 18

In you, O LORD, I have taken refuge; let me never be put to shame. Rescue me and deliver me in your righteousness; turn your ear to me and save me. Be my rock of refuge, to which I can always go; give the command to save me, for you are my rock and my fortress. Deliver me, O my God, from the hand of the wicked, from the grasp of evil and cruel men.

For you have been my hope, O Sovereign LORD, my confidence since my youth. From birth I have relied on you; you brought me forth from my mother's womb. I will ever praise you.

Since my youth, O God, you have taught me, and to this day I declare your marvelous deeds. Even when I am old and gray, do not forsake me, O God, till I declare your power to the next generation, your might to all who are to come.

GOSPEL READING
John 14:15–17

"If you love me, you will obey what I command. And I will ask the Father, and he will give you another Counselor to be with you forever—the Spirit of truth. The world cannot accept him, because it neither sees him nor knows him. But you know him, for he lives with you and will be in you.

SPACE FOR REFLECTION

CLOSING PRAYERS
Lord, have mercy.
Christ, have mercy.
Lord, have mercy.

Our Father, who art in heaven. . . .

Lord, hear my prayer.
And let my cry come unto you.

COLLECT

Almighty God our heavenly Father, whose grace here on earth brings us the gifts of heaven, guide us in this present life, and so lead us now, that we might dwell in the light of your eternal love. We ask this through our Lord Jesus Christ your Son, who lives and reigns with you and the Holy Spirit, one God forever and ever. Amen.

Lord, hear my prayer.
And let my cry come unto you.
Let us bless the Lord.
Thanks be to God.

May the souls of the faithful
by the mercy of God rest in peace.
Amen.
May divine help always be with us.
And with those who are absent from us.
Amen.

WEEK 4

MORNING PRAYER

Sunday
Week 4

O Lord, open my lips.
And my mouth will proclaim your praise.

OPENING PRAYER

May our compassionate God drive away all
our anguish, bestow health, and give us by
the loving-kindness of the Father, the kingdom of the heavens. Amen.

PSALM 27:1–5

The LORD is my light and my salvation—
whom shall I fear? The LORD is the stronghold
of my life—of whom shall I be afraid? When
evil men advance against me to devour my
flesh, when my enemies and my foes attack
me, they will stumble and fall. Though an
army besiege me, my heart will not fear;
though war break out against me, even then
will I be confident.

One thing I ask of the LORD, this is
what I seek: that I may dwell in the house of
the LORD all the days of my life, to gaze upon

the beauty of the LORD and to seek him in his temple. For in the day of trouble he will keep me safe in his dwelling; he will hide me in the shelter of his tabernacle and set me high upon a rock.

READING
Margaret Silf

Every situation in our lives has a "high cross" somewhere within it. Day after day, over and over, we find ourselves sensing that unease inside which warns us we are not living true to the core of our being. But just as certainly, day by day we will find, if we keep our eyes open, the traces of "forever moments."

SPACE FOR REFLECTION

BENEDICTUS
Canticle of Zechariah: Luke 1:68–79

"Praise be to the Lord, the God of Israel, because he has come and has redeemed his people. He has raised up a horn of salvation for us in the house of his servant David (as he said through his holy prophets of long ago), salvation from our enemies and from the hand of all who hate us—to show mercy to our fathers and to remember his holy covenant, the oath he swore to our father Abraham: to rescue us from the hand of our enemies, and to enable us to serve him without fear in holiness and righteousness before him all our days.

And you, my child, will be called a prophet of the Most High; for you will go on before the Lord to prepare the way for him, to give his people the knowledge of salvation through the forgiveness of their sins, because of the tender mercy of our God, by which the rising sun will come to us from heaven to shine on those living in darkness and in the shadow of death, to guide our feet into the path of peace."

CLOSING PRAYERS
Lord, have mercy.
Christ, have mercy.
Lord, have mercy.

Our Father, who art in heaven. . . .

Lord, hear my prayer.
And let my cry come unto you.

COLLECT
Lord God and merciful Father, you stand by your people on whom you have bestowed the gift of faith. Grant them your sure presence in this world, and their eternal heritage in the world to come. We ask this through our Lord

Jesus Christ your Son, who lives and reigns with you and the Holy Spirit, one God forever and ever. Amen.

Lord, hear my prayer.
And let my cry come unto you.
Let us bless the Lord.
Thanks be to God.

May the souls of the faithful
by the mercy of God rest in peace.
Amen.
May divine help always be with us.
And with those who are absent from us.
Amen.

MIDDAY SERVICE

Sunday
Week 4

O God, come to my assistance.
O Lord, make haste to help me.

OPENING PRAYER

Mighty Ruler, true God, you who regulate the functions of all things and provide the morning its splendor, the midday its heat. Extinguish the flames of quarrels, take away harmful passions, grant healing of body and true peace of heart. Amen.

PSALM 119:113–120

I hate double-minded men, but I love your law. You are my refuge and my shield; I have put my hope in your word. Away from me, you evildoers, that I may keep the commands of my God! Sustain me according to your promise, and I will live; do not let my hopes be dashed. Uphold me, and I will be delivered; I will always have regard for your decrees. You reject all who stray from your decrees, for their deceitfulness is in vain. All the wicked of the earth you discard like dross; therefore I love your statutes. My flesh trembles in fear of you; I stand in awe of your laws.

SPACE FOR REFLECTION

CLOSING PRAYERS
Let your mercy, O Lord, be upon us.
As we have hoped in you.

Lord, have mercy.
Christ, have mercy.
Lord, have mercy.

Our Father, who art in heaven. . . .

Lord, hear my prayer.
And let my cry come unto you.
Let us bless the Lord.
Thanks be to God.
May divine help always be with us.
And with those who are absent from us.
Amen.

VESPERS

Sunday
Week 4

O God, come to my assistance.
O Lord, make haste to help me.

OPENING PRAYER

O Light, blessed Trinity and perfect Unity, already the fiery sun is receding; pour the light of your presence into our hearts. Amen.

PSALM 126

When the LORD brought back the captives to Zion, we were like men who dreamed. Our mouths were filled with laughter, our tongues with songs of joy. Then it was said among the nations, "The LORD has done great things for them." The LORD has done great things for us, and we are filled with joy.

Restore our fortunes, O LORD, like streams in the Negev. Those who sow in tears will reap with songs of joy. He who goes out weeping, carrying seed to sow, will return with songs of joy, carrying sheaves with him.

GOSPEL READING
John 14:18–19

"I will not leave you as orphans; I will come to you. Before long, the world will not see me anymore, but you will see me. Because I live, you also will live."

SPACE FOR REFLECTION

MAGNIFICAT
The Canticle of Mary: Luke 1:46b–55

"My soul glorifies the Lord, and my spirit rejoices in God my Savior, for he has been mindful of the humble state of his servant. From now on all generations will call me blessed, for the Mighty One has done great things for me—holy is his name.

His mercy extends to those who fear him, from generation to generation. He has performed mighty deeds with his arm; he has scattered those who are proud in their inmost thoughts. He has brought down rulers from their thrones but has lifted up the humble. He has filled the hungry with good things but has sent the rich away empty. He has helped his servant Israel, remembering to be merciful to Abraham and his descendants forever, even as he said to our fathers."

CLOSING PRAYERS
Lord, have mercy.
Christ, have mercy.
Lord, have mercy.

Our Father, who art in heaven. . . .

Lord, hear my prayer.
And let my cry come unto you.

COLLECT
Lord God and merciful Father, you stand by
your people on whom you have bestowed the
gift of faith. Grant them your sure presence
in this world, and their eternal heritage in the
world to come. We pray this in the name of
our Lord and Savior Jesus Christ. Amen.

Lord, hear my prayer.
And let my cry come unto you.
Let us bless the Lord.
Thanks be to God.

May the souls of the faithful
by the mercy of God rest in peace.
Amen.
May divine help always be with us.
And with those who are absent from us.
Amen.

MORNING PRAYER

Monday
Week 4

O Lord, open my lips.
And my mouth will proclaim your praise.

OPENING PRAYER
Lord Jesus, Splendor of the Father's glory, O true Sun, descend, sparkling with uninterrupted brightness; O radiance of the Holy Spirit, pour in upon our senses. Amen.

PSALM 82
God presides in the great assembly; he gives judgment among the "gods": "How long will you defend the unjust and show partiality to the wicked? Defend the cause of the weak and fatherless; maintain the rights of the poor and oppressed. Rescue the weak and needy; deliver them from the hand of the wicked.

"They know nothing, they understand nothing. They walk about in darkness; all the foundations of the earth are shaken.

"I said, 'You are "gods"; you are all sons of the Most High.' But you will die like mere men; you will fall like every other ruler."

Rise up, O God, judge the earth, for all the nations are your inheritance.

READING
Antony the Great

"What must one do in order to please God?" Antony replied, "Pay attention to what I tell you. Whoever you may be, always have God before your eyes. Whatever you do, do it according to the testimony of the holy Scriptures. Wherever you live, do not easily leave it. Keep these three precepts and you will be saved."

SPACE FOR REFLECTION

CLOSING PRAYERS
Lord, have mercy.
Christ, have mercy.
Lord, have mercy.

Our Father, who art in heaven. . . .

Lord, hear my prayer.
And let my cry come unto you.

COLLECT

Almighty, ever-living God, through Christ your Son you made of us a new creation. Shape us in his likeness, since he has brought our human nature to you. We ask this through the same Jesus Christ your Son, who lives and reigns with you and the Holy Spirit, one God, forever and ever. Amen.

Lord, hear my prayer.
And let my cry come unto you.
Let us bless the Lord.
Thanks be to God.

May the souls of the faithful
by the mercy of God rest in peace.
Amen.
May divine help always be with us.
And with those who are absent from us.
Amen.

MIDDAY SERVICE

Monday
Week 4

O God, come to my assistance.
O Lord, make haste to help me.

OPENING PRAYER

O Christ, you are the Light, the Splendor of the Father, and the eternal Hope of all things. Listen to the prayers which your servants throughout the world pour forth. Amen.

PSALM 119:121–128

I have done what is righteous and just; do not leave me to my oppressors. Ensure your servant's well-being; let not the arrogant oppress me. My eyes fail, looking for your salvation, looking for your righteous promise. Deal with your servant according to your love and teach me your decrees. I am your servant; give me discernment that I may understand your statutes. It is time for you to act, O LORD; your law is being broken. Because I love your commands more than gold, more than pure gold, and because I consider all your precepts right, I hate every wrong path.

SPACE FOR REFLECTION

CLOSING PRAYERS

Let your mercy, O Lord, be upon us.
As we have hoped in you.

Lord, have mercy.
Christ, have mercy.
Lord, have mercy.

Our Father, who art in heaven. . . .

Lord, hear my prayer.
And let my cry come unto you.
Let us bless the Lord.
Thanks be to God.
May divine help always be with us.
And with those who are absent from us.
Amen.

VESPERS

Monday
Week 4

O God, come to my assistance.
O Lord, make haste to help me.

OPENING PRAYER
Pour into us now, O most loving One, the
gift of eternal grace, so that, by the misfortunes
of new deception, old error may not destroy
us. Amen.

PSALM 107:1–9
Give thanks to the LORD, for he is good; his
love endures forever. Let the redeemed of the
LORD say this—those he redeemed from the
hand of the foe, those he gathered from the
lands, from east and west, from north and
south.

Some wandered in desert wastelands,
finding no way to a city where they could
settle. They were hungry and thirsty, and
their lives ebbed away. Then they cried out
to the LORD in their trouble, and he delivered them from their distress. He led them
by a straight way to a city where they could
settle. Let them give thanks to the LORD for

his unfailing love and his wonderful deeds for men, for he satisfies the thirsty and fills the hungry with good things.

GOSPEL READING
John 18:4–6

Jesus, knowing all that was going to happen to him, went out and asked them, "Who is it you want?"

"Jesus of Nazareth," they replied.

"I am he," Jesus said. (And Judas the traitor was standing there with them.) When Jesus said, "I am he," they drew back and fell to the ground.

SPACE FOR REFLECTION

CLOSING PRAYERS
Lord, have mercy.
Christ, have mercy.
Lord, have mercy.

Our Father, who art in heaven. . . .

Lord, hear my prayer.
And let my cry come unto you.

COLLECT

Almighty, ever-living God, through Christ your Son you made of us a new creation. Shape us in his likeness, since he has brought our human nature to you. We ask this through the same Jesus Christ your Son, who lives and reigns with you and the Holy Spirit, one God, forever and ever. Amen.

Lord, hear my prayer.
And let my cry come unto you.
Let us bless the Lord.
Thanks be to God.

May the souls of the faithful
by the mercy of God rest in peace.
Amen.
May divine help always be with us.
And with those who are absent from us.
Amen.

MORNING PRAYER

Tuesday
Week 4

O Lord, open my lips.
And my mouth will proclaim your praise.

OPENING PRAYER
O Christ, dispel sleep, break the chains of night, release long-standing sin, and pour in new light. Amen.

PSALM 96:1–9
Sing to the LORD a new song; sing to the LORD, all the earth. Sing to the LORD, praise his name; proclaim his salvation day after day. Declare his glory among the nations, his marvelous deeds among all peoples.

For great is the LORD and most worthy of praise; he is to be feared above all gods. For all the gods of the nations are idols, but the LORD made the heavens. Splendor and majesty are before him; strength and glory are in his sanctuary.

Ascribe to the LORD, O families of nations, ascribe to the LORD glory and strength. Ascribe to the LORD the glory due his name; bring an offering and come into his courts. Worship the LORD in the splendor of his holiness; tremble before him, all the earth.

READING
John of the Cross

The will cannot contain within itself both passion for created things and passion for God. What does the created thing have to do with the Creator? What does the sensual have to do with the spiritual? The visible with the invisible? The temporal with the eternal?

SPACE FOR REFLECTION

CLOSING PRAYERS

Lord, have mercy.
Christ, have mercy.
Lord, have mercy.

Our Father, who art in heaven. . . .

Lord, hear my prayer.
And let my cry come unto you.

COLLECT

Eternal and omnipotent God, you have called us to be members of one body. Join us with those who in all times and places have praised your name, that with one heart and mind, we may show the unity of your church, and bring honor to our Lord and Savior. We ask this through the same Jesus Christ your Son, who lives and reigns with you and the Holy Spirit, one God forever and ever. Amen.

Lord, hear my prayer.
And let my cry come unto you.
Let us bless the Lord.
Thanks be to God.

May the souls of the faithful
by the mercy of God rest in peace.
Amen.
May divine help always be with us.
And with those who are absent from us.
Amen.

MIDDAY
SERVICE

Tuesday
Week 4

O God, come to my assistance.
O Lord, make haste to help me.

OPENING PRAYER

O Jesus, our redemption, love, and desire, may your love constrain you to pass over our evils, sparing us, and having answered our prayer, may you satisfy us with your face. Amen.

PSALM 119:129–136

Your statutes are wonderful; therefore I obey them. The unfolding of your words gives light; it gives understanding to the simple. I open my mouth and pant, longing for your commands. Turn to me and have mercy on me, as you always do to those who love your name. Direct my footsteps according to your word; let no sin rule over me. Redeem me from the oppression of men, that I may obey your precepts. Make your face shine upon your servant and teach me your decrees.

Streams of tears flow from my eyes, for your law is not obeyed.

SPACE FOR REFLECTION

CLOSING PRAYERS
Let your mercy, O Lord, be upon us.
As we have hoped in you.

Lord, have mercy.
Christ, have mercy.
Lord, have mercy.

Our Father, who art in heaven. . . .

Lord, hear my prayer.
And let my cry come unto you.
Let us bless the Lord.
Thanks be to God.
May divine help always be with us.
And with those who are absent from us.
Amen.

VESPERS

Tuesday
Week 4

O God, come to my assistance.
O Lord, make haste to help me.

OPENING PRAYER

O great Creator of the earth, cleanse the wounds of our souls with the freshness of your grace, destroy wrong impulses, and let us be filled with your good things. Amen.

PSALM 114

When Israel came out of Egypt, the house of Jacob from a people of foreign tongue, Judah became God's sanctuary, Israel his dominion.

The sea looked and fled, the Jordan turned back; the mountains skipped like rams, the hills like lambs.

Why was it, O sea, that you fled, O Jordan, that you turned back, you mountains, that you skipped like rams, you hills, like lambs?

Tremble, O earth, at the presence of the Lord, at the presence of the God of Jacob, who turned the rock into a pool, the hard rock into springs of water.

GOSPEL READING
John 18:37–38a

"You are a king, then!" said Pilate.

Jesus answered, "You are right in saying I am a king. In fact, for this reason I was born, and for this I came into the world, to testify to the truth. Everyone on the side of the truth listens to me."

"What is truth?" Pilate asked.

SPACE FOR REFLECTION

CLOSING PRAYERS
Lord, have mercy.
Christ, have mercy.
Lord, have mercy.

Our Father, who art in heaven. . . .

Lord, hear my prayer.
And let my cry come unto you.

COLLECT

Eternal and omnipotent God, you have called us to be members of one body. Join us with those who in all times and places have praised your name, that with one heart and mind, we may show the unity of your church, and bring honor to our Lord and Savior. We ask this through the same Jesus Christ your

Son, who lives and reigns with you and the
Holy Spirit, one God forever and ever. Amen.

Lord, hear my prayer.
And let my cry come unto you.
Let us bless the Lord.
Thanks be to God.

May the souls of the faithful
by the mercy of God rest in peace.
Amen.
May divine help always be with us.
And with those who are absent from us.
Amen.

MORNING PRAYER

Wednesday
Week 4

O Lord, open my lips.
And my mouth will proclaim your praise.

OPENING PRAYER

To you, O Christ, King most loving, and to the Father be glory with the Spirit, the Paraclete, for everlasting ages. Amen.

PSALM 92:1–7, 12–15

It is good to praise the LORD and make music to your name, O Most High, to proclaim your love in the morning and your faithfulness at night, to the music of the ten-stringed lyre and the melody of the harp.

For you make me glad by your deeds, O LORD; I sing for joy at the works of your hands. How great are your works, O LORD, how profound your thoughts! The senseless man does not know, fools do not understand, that though the wicked spring up like grass and all evildoers flourish, they will be forever destroyed.

The righteous will flourish like a palm tree, they will grow like a cedar of Lebanon; planted in the house of the LORD, they will flourish in the courts of our God. They will still bear fruit in old age, they will stay fresh and green, proclaiming, "The LORD is upright; he is my Rock, and there is no wickedness in him."

READING
Cindy Crosby

Our soul longs to speak. Isn't this offering up of our creativity a prayer in itself? Our soul speaking in paint, in words, in landscape? An attempt to open a window between us and something greater than ourselves that we dimly perceive, try to express?

SPACE FOR REFLECTION

CLOSING PRAYERS
Lord, have mercy.
Christ, have mercy.
Lord, have mercy.

Our Father, who art in heaven. . . .

Lord, hear my prayer.
And let my cry come unto you.

COLLECT

Almighty and loving God, your Son came into the world to free us all from sin and death. Breathe upon us the power of your Spirit, that we may be raised to new life in Christ and serve you in holiness and right-eousness all our days. We ask this through our Lord Jesus Christ your Son. Amen.

Lord, hear my prayer.
And let my cry come unto you.
Let us bless the Lord.
Thanks be to God.

May the souls of the faithful
by the mercy of God rest in peace.
Amen.
May divine help always be with us.
And with those who are absent from us.
Amen.

MIDDAY SERVICE

Wednesday
Week 4

O God, come to my assistance.
O Lord, make haste to help me.

OPENING PRAYER
Jesus, Lord God and Creator of all things, be yourself our joy, you who are the future prize. May our glory be in you always, through all the ages. Amen.

PSALM 119:137–144
Righteous are you, O LORD, and your laws are right. The statutes you have laid down are righteous; they are fully trustworthy. My zeal wears me out, for my enemies ignore your words. Your promises have been thoroughly tested, and your servant loves them. Though I am lowly and despised, I do not forget your precepts. Your righteousness is everlasting and your law is true. Trouble and distress have come upon me, but your commands are my delight. Your statutes are forever right; give me understanding that I may live.

SPACE FOR REFLECTION

CLOSING PRAYERS

Let your mercy, O Lord, be upon us.
As we have hoped in you.

Lord, have mercy.
Christ, have mercy.
Lord, have mercy.

Our Father, who art in heaven. . . .

Lord, hear my prayer.
And let my cry come unto you.
Let us bless the Lord.
Thanks be to God.
May divine help always be with us.
And with those who are absent from us.
Amen.

VESPERS

Wednesday
Week 4

O God, come to my assistance.
O Lord, make haste to help me.

OPENING PRAYER

Most holy God of heaven, you who paint the shining center of the sky with the brightness of fire, illumine our hearts, banish sordid things, release the chain of guilt, and make void our crimes. Amen.

PSALM 139:1, 2, 6–12

O LORD, you have searched me and you know me. You know when I sit and when I rise; you perceive my thoughts from afar.

Such knowledge is too wonderful for me, too lofty for me to attain.

Where can I go from your Spirit? Where can I flee from your presence? If I go up to the heavens, you are there; if I make my bed in the depths, you are there. If I rise on the wings of the dawn, if I settle on the far side of the sea, even there your hand will guide me, your right hand will hold me fast.

If I say, "Surely the darkness will hide me and the light become night around me," even the darkness will not be dark to you; the night will shine like the day, for darkness is as light to you.

GOSPEL READING
John 19:1–3

Then Pilate took Jesus and had him flogged. The soldiers twisted together a crown of thorns and put it on his head. They clothed him in a purple robe and went up to him again and again, saying, "Hail, king of the Jews!" And they struck him in the face.

SPACE FOR REFLECTION

CLOSING PRAYERS

Lord, have mercy.
Christ, have mercy.
Lord, have mercy.

Our Father, who art in heaven. . . .

Lord, hear my prayer.
And let my cry come unto you.

COLLECT

Almighty and loving God, your Son came into the world to free us all from sin and death. Breathe upon us the power of your Spirit, that we may be raised to new life in Christ and serve you in holiness and righteousness all our days. We ask this through the same Jesus Christ your Son, who lives and reigns with you and the Holy Spirit, one God forever and ever. Amen.

Lord, hear my prayer.
And let my cry come unto you.
Let us bless the Lord.
Thanks be to God.

May the souls of the faithful
by the mercy of God rest in peace.
Amen.
May divine help always be with us.
And with those who are absent from us.
Amen.

MORNING PRAYER

Thursday
Week 4

O Lord, open my lips.
And my mouth will proclaim your praise.

OPENING PRAYER

Behold, the fiery sun is rising; may blindness at last depart—let us speak nothing underhanded, let us consider nothing dark. To God the Father be glory, and to his only Son, with the Spirit, the Paraclete, for everlasting ages. Amen.

PSALM 98:1–3, 7–9

Sing to the LORD a new song, for he has done marvelous things; his right hand and his holy arm have worked salvation for him. The LORD has made his salvation known and revealed his righteousness to the nations. He has remembered his love and his faithfulness to the house of Israel; all the ends of the earth have seen the salvation of our God.

Let the sea resound, and everything in it, the world, and all who live in it. Let the rivers clap their hands, let the mountains sing together for joy; let them sing before the LORD, for he comes to judge the earth. He will judge the world in righteousness and the peoples with equity.

READING
M. Basil Pennington, O.C.S.O.
We drink the cup of salvation, the precious blood of the Lord, which poured forth from his side when he slept the sleep of death upon the cross, but which he had already given us in sacramental mystery the night before in the cup of the new covenant. Signed with this saving blood, we are safe.

SPACE FOR REFLECTION

CLOSING PRAYERS
Lord, have mercy.
Christ, have mercy.
Lord, have mercy.

Our Father, who art in heaven. . . .

Lord, hear my prayer.
And let my cry come unto you.

COLLECT

Almighty and merciful God, your Son fasted forty days in the wilderness and was tempted as we, but without sin. Give us grace to direct our lives in obedience to your Spirit, that we may know your power to save. We ask this through the same Jesus Christ your Son, who lives and reigns with you and the Holy Spirit, one God forever and ever. Amen.

Lord, hear my prayer.
And let my cry come unto you.
Let us bless the Lord.
Thanks be to God.

May the souls of the faithful
by the mercy of God rest in peace.
Amen.
May divine help always be with us.
And with those who are absent from us.
Amen.

MIDDAY
SERVICE

Thursday
Week 4

O God, come to my assistance.
O Lord, make haste to help me.

OPENING PRAYER
Come, Creator Spirit, Paraclete, gift of God most high, visit the souls of your people, and fill with supernal grace the hearts which you created. Amen.

PSALM 119:145–152
I call with all my heart; answer me, O LORD, and I will obey your decrees. I call out to you; save me and I will keep your statutes. I rise before dawn and cry for help; I have put my hope in your word. My eyes stay open through the watches of the night, that I may meditate on your promises. Hear my voice in accordance with your love; preserve my life, O LORD, according to your laws. Those who devise wicked schemes are near, but they are far from your law. Yet you are near, O LORD, and all your commands are true. Long ago I

learned from your statutes that you established them to last forever.

SPACE FOR REFLECTION

CLOSING PRAYERS
Let your mercy, O Lord, be upon us.
As we have hoped in you.

Lord, have mercy.
Christ, have mercy.
Lord, have mercy.

Our Father, who art in heaven. . . .

Lord, hear my prayer.
And let my cry come unto you.
Let us bless the Lord.
Thanks be to God.
May divine help always be with us.
And with those who are absent from us.
Amen.

VESPERS

Thursday
Week 4

OPENING PRAYER

O God of great power, you have rescued us from error and from the weariness of death. We give you thanks and praise. Amen.

PSALM 139:13–18, 23, 24

For you created my inmost being; you knit me together in my mother's womb. I praise you because I am fearfully and wonderfully made; your works are wonderful, I know that full well. My frame was not hidden from you when I was made in the secret place. When I was woven together in the depths of the earth, your eyes saw my unformed body. All the days ordained for me were written in your book before one of them came to be.

How precious to me are your thoughts, O God! How vast is the sum of them! Were I to count them, they would outnumber the grains of sand. When I awake, I am still with you.

Search me, O God, and know my heart; test me and know my anxious thoughts. See if there is any offensive way in me, and lead me in the way everlasting.

GOSPEL READING
John 19:16–19
Finally Pilate handed him over to be crucified.

So the soldiers took charge of Jesus. Carrying his own cross, he went out to the place of the skull. . . . Here they crucified him, and with him two others—one on each side and Jesus in the middle.

Pilate had a notice prepared and fastened to the cross. It read: JESUS OF NAZARETH, THE KING OF THE JEWS.

SPACE FOR REFLECTION

CLOSING PRAYERS
Lord, have mercy.
Christ, have mercy.
Lord, have mercy.

Our Father, who art in heaven. . . .

Lord, hear my prayer.
And let my cry come unto you.

COLLECT

Almighty and merciful God, your Son fasted forty days in the wilderness and was tempted as we, but without sin. Give us grace to direct our lives in obedience to your Spirit, that we may know your power to save. We ask this through our Lord Jesus Christ your Son. Amen.

Lord, hear my prayer.
And let my cry come unto you.
Let us bless the Lord.
Thanks be to God.

May the souls of the faithful
by the mercy of God rest in peace.
Amen.
May divine help always be with us.
And with those who are absent from us.
Amen.

MORNING PRAYER

Friday
Week 4

O Lord, open my lips.
And my mouth will proclaim your praise.

OPENING PRAYER

O eternal Glory of heaven, blessed Hope of mortals, give your right hand to those who are getting up; let the soul arise sober and, ardent in praise, returning thanks to you. Amen.

PSALM 51:1–13

Have mercy on me, O God, according to your unfailing love; according to your great compassion blot out my transgressions. Wash away all my iniquity and cleanse me from my sin.

For I know my transgressions, and my sin is always before me. Against you, you only, have I sinned and done what is evil in your sight, so that you are proved right when you speak and justified when you judge. Surely I was sinful at birth, sinful from the time my mother conceived me. Surely you desire truth in the inner parts; you teach me wisdom in the inmost place.

Cleanse me with hyssop, and I will be clean; wash me, and I will be whiter than snow. Let me hear joy and gladness; let the bones you have crushed rejoice. Hide your face from my sins and blot out all my iniquity.

Create in me a pure heart, O God, and renew a steadfast spirit within me. Do not cast me from your presence or take your Holy Spirit from me. Restore to me the joy of your salvation and grant me a willing spirit, to sustain me.

Then I will teach transgressors your ways, and sinners will turn back to you.

READING
George Herbert
All you who pass by, whose eyes and mind to worldly things are sharp, but to me blind, to me who took eyes that I might you find: was ever grief like mine?

SPACE FOR REFLECTION

CLOSING PRAYERS
Lord, have mercy.
Christ, have mercy.
Lord, have mercy.

Our Father, who art in heaven. . . .

Lord, hear my prayer.
And let my cry come unto you.

COLLECT
Almighty God, heavenly Father, you are the
source and end of all good. Inspire us with
good intentions, and by the power of your
Spirit help us to fulfill them, to your honor
and glory. We ask this through our Lord Jesus
Christ your Son. Amen.

Lord, hear my prayer.
And let my cry come unto you.
Let us bless the Lord.
Thanks be to God.

May the souls of the faithful
by the mercy of God rest in peace.
Amen.
May divine help always be with us.
And with those who are absent from us.
Amen.

MIDDAY SERVICE

Friday
Week 4

O God, come to my assistance.
O Lord, make haste to help me.

OPENING PRAYER

Come, Holy Spirit, kindle light for our senses,
pour out love in our hearts, and undergird
with perpetual strength the weaknesses of our
body. Amen.

PSALM 119:153–160

Look upon my suffering and deliver me, for I
have not forgotten your law. Defend my
cause and redeem me; preserve my life
according to your promise. Salvation is far
from the wicked, for they do not seek out
your decrees. Your compassion is great, O
LORD; preserve my life according to your
laws. Many are the foes who persecute me,
but I have not turned from your statutes. I
look on the faithless with loathing, for they
do not obey your word. See how I love your
precepts; preserve my life, O LORD, according

to your love. All your words are true; all your righteous laws are eternal.

SPACE FOR REFLECTION

CLOSING PRAYERS

Let your mercy, O Lord, be upon us.
As we have hoped in you.

Lord, have mercy.
Christ, have mercy.
Lord, have mercy.

Our Father, who art in heaven. . . .

Lord, hear my prayer.
And let my cry come unto you.
Let us bless the Lord.
Thanks be to God.
May divine help always be with us.
And with those who are absent from us.
Amen.

VESPERS

Friday
Week 4

O God, come to my assistance.
O Lord, make haste to help me.

OPENING PRAYER

O God, Maker of all mankind, give the rewards of joy, grant the gifts of graces, dissolve the chains of quarreling, and bind fast the agreements of peace. Amen.

PSALM 142

I cry aloud to the LORD; I lift up my voice to the LORD for mercy. I pour out my complaint before him; before him I tell my trouble.

When my spirit grows faint within me, it is you who know my way. In the path where I walk men have hidden a snare for me. Look to my right and see; no one is concerned for me. I have no refuge; no one cares for my life.

I cry to you, O LORD; I say, "You are my refuge, my portion in the land of the living." Listen to my cry, for I am in desperate need; rescue me from those who pursue me, for they are too strong for me. Set me free from my prison, that I may praise your name.

Then the righteous will gather about me
because of your goodness to me.

GOSPEL READING
John 20:19–20

On the evening of that first day of the week,
when the disciples were together, with the
doors locked for fear of the Jews, Jesus came
and stood among them and said, "Peace be
with you!" After he said this, he showed them
his hands and side. The disciples were over-
joyed when they saw the Lord.

SPACE FOR REFLECTION

CLOSING PRAYERS

Lord, have mercy.
Christ, have mercy.
Lord, have mercy.

Our Father, who art in heaven. . . .

Lord, hear my prayer.
And let my cry come unto you.

COLLECT

Almighty God, heavenly Father, you are the source and end of all good. Inspire us with good intentions, and by the power of your Spirit help us to fulfill them, to your honor and glory. We ask this through our Lord Jesus Christ your Son, who lives and reigns with you and the Holy Spirit, one God forever and ever. Amen.

Lord, hear my prayer.
And let my cry come unto you.
Let us bless the Lord.
Thanks be to God.

May the souls of the faithful
by the mercy of God rest in peace.
Amen.
May divine help always be with us.
And with those who are absent from us.
Amen.

MORNING PRAYER

Saturday
Week 4

O Lord, open my lips.
And my mouth will proclaim your praise.

OPENING PRAYER

O Light, shine on our senses and dispel the sleep of our soul. To you before all else let our voice resound, and let us pay our vows to you. Amen.

PSALM 32:1–7

Blessed is he whose transgressions are forgiven, whose sins are covered. Blessed is the man whose sin the LORD does not count against him and in whose spirit is no deceit.

When I kept silent, my bones wasted away through my groaning all day long. For day and night your hand was heavy upon me; my strength was sapped as in the heat of summer.

Then I acknowledged my sin to you and did not cover up my iniquity. I said, "I will confess my transgressions to the LORD"— and you forgave the guilt of my sin. Therefore let everyone who is godly pray to you while you may be found; surely when the mighty waters rise, they will not reach him. You are my hiding place; you will protect me from trouble and surround me with songs of deliverance.

READING
François Fénelon
How can we expect to find Jesus if we do not seek him in the states of this earthly life, in loneliness and silence, in poverty and suffering, in persecution and contempt, in annihilation and the cross?

SPACE FOR REFLECTION

CLOSING PRAYERS
Lord, have mercy.
Christ, have mercy.
Lord, have mercy.

Our Father, who art in heaven. . . .

Lord, hear my prayer.
And let my cry come unto you.

COLLECT

Father of all humanity, you call your children to walk in the light of Christ. Free us from darkness and keep us forever in the radiance of your truth, until we come at last to live with you on high. We ask this through our Lord Jesus Christ your Son, who lives and reigns with you and the Holy Spirit, one God forever and ever. Amen.

Lord, hear my prayer.
And let my cry come unto you.
Let us bless the Lord.
Thanks be to God.

May the souls of the faithful
by the mercy of God rest in peace.
Amen.
May divine help always be with us.
And with those who are absent from us.
Amen.

MIDDAY
SERVICE

Saturday
Week 4

O God, come to my assistance.
O Lord, make haste to help me.

OPENING PRAYER

Grant us a wholesome life, revive our zeal and love, O Father Almighty, through Jesus Christ the Lord, who reigns with you for all time with the Holy Spirit. Amen.

PSALM 119:161–168

Rulers persecute me without cause, but my heart trembles at your word. I rejoice in your promise like one who finds great spoil. I hate and abhor falsehood but I love your law. Seven times a day I praise you for your righteous laws. Great peace have they who love your law, and nothing can make them stumble. I wait for your salvation, O LORD, and I follow your commands. I obey your statutes, for I love them greatly. I obey your precepts and your statutes, for all my ways are known to you.

SPACE FOR REFLECTION

CLOSING PRAYERS

Let your mercy, O Lord, be upon us.
As we have hoped in you.

Lord, have mercy.
Christ, have mercy.
Lord, have mercy.

Our Father, who art in heaven. . . .

Lord, hear my prayer.
And let my cry come unto you.
Let us bless the Lord.
Thanks be to God.
May divine help always be with us.
And with those who are absent from us.
Amen.

VESPERS

Saturday
Week 4

O God, come to my assistance.
O Lord, make haste to help me.

OPENING PRAYER

O God, Creator of all things and Ruler of heaven, we give thanks for the day that is finished and we pray at the start of the night. May faith not know darkness; may the night shine with faith. Amen.

PSALM 112:1–7

Praise the LORD. Blessed is the man who fears the LORD, who finds great delight in his commands. His children will be mighty in the land; the generation of the upright will be blessed. Wealth and riches are in his house, and his righteousness endures forever. Even in darkness light dawns for the upright, for the gracious and compassionate and righteous man. Good will come to him who is generous and lends freely, who conducts his affairs with justice. Surely he will never be shaken; a righteous man will be remembered forever.

He will have no fear of bad news; his heart is steadfast, trusting in the LORD.

GOSPEL READING
John 20:30, 31

Jesus did many other miraculous signs in the presence of his disciples, which are not recorded in this book. But these are written that you may believe that Jesus is the Christ, the Son of God, and that by believing you may have life in his name.

SPACE FOR REFLECTION

CLOSING PRAYERS
Lord, have mercy.
Christ, have mercy.
Lord, have mercy.

Our Father, who art in heaven. . . .

Lord, hear my prayer.
And let my cry come unto you.

COLLECT

Father of all humanity, you call your children to walk in the light of Christ. Free us from darkness and keep us forever in the radiance of your truth, until we come at last to live with you on high. We pray this in the name of our Lord and Savior Jesus Christ. Amen.

Lord, hear my prayer.
And let my cry come unto you.
Let us bless the Lord.
Thanks be to God.

May the souls of the faithful
by the mercy of God rest in peace.
Amen.
May divine help always be with us.
And with those who are absent from us.
Amen.

COMPLINE

COMPLINE

O God, come to my assistance.
O Lord, make haste to help me.

OPENING PRAYER

May our hearts dream of you, sense your
presence in deep sleep, and always sing your
glory with the approaching light. Amen.

CONFESSION

I confess to God Almighty, the Father, the
Son, and the Holy Spirit, that I have sinned
in thought, word, and deed through my own
grievous fault. Therefore, I pray God to have
mercy on me. Almighty God, have mercy
upon us, forgive us all our sins and deliver us
from all evil; confirm and strengthen us in all
goodness, and bring us to life everlasting;
through Jesus Christ our Lord. Amen.

PSALM 4

Answer me when I call to you, O my righteous
God. Give me relief from my distress; be
merciful to me and hear my prayer.

How long, O men, will you turn my glory into shame? How long will you love delusions and seek false gods? Know that the LORD has set apart the godly for himself; the LORD will hear when I call to him.

In your anger do not sin; when you are on your beds, search your hearts and be silent. Offer right sacrifices and trust in the LORD.

Many are asking, "Who can show us any good?" Let the light of your face shine upon us, O LORD. You have filled my heart with greater joy than when their grain and new wine abound. I will lie down and sleep in peace, for you alone, O LORD, make me dwell in safety.

CLOSING PRAYERS
Into your hands, O Lord,
I commend my spirit.
For you have redeemed us, Lord,
O God of truth.

Lord, have mercy.
Christ, have mercy.
Lord, have mercy.

Our Father, who art in heaven. . . .

Lord, hear my prayer.
And let my cry come unto you.
Let us bless the Lord.
Thanks be to God.

May divine help always be with us.
And with those who are absent from us.
Amen.

PRAYERS
FOR VARIOUS OCCASIONS

IN THE MORNING

Heavenly Father, your steadfast love never ceases; your mercies never end, but are new every morning. We raise our hearts to you and ask you to go before us throughout this day. May we follow step by step with hearts that are steadfast and unafraid. By your grace, bring us to evening time grateful that we have spent the day under your protection. In Jesus' name. Amen.

IN THE EVENING

O God, whose love knows no rising or setting, we thank you for your care in the day now ending. Forgive us for all we have done amiss, and send your peace into our hearts. Protect us from all danger and harm throughout this night, for Jesus Christ our Savior's sake. Amen.

(The following are taken from
The Book of Common Prayer *1979, Episcopal Church USA)*

FOR JOY IN GOD'S CREATION

O heavenly Father, who hast filled the world with beauty: Open our eyes to behold thy gracious hand in all thy works; that, rejoicing in thy whole creation, we may learn to serve thee with gladness; for the sake of him through whom all things were made, thy Son Jesus Christ our Lord. Amen.

FOR THE HUMAN FAMILY

O God, you made us in your own image and redeemed us through Jesus your Son: Look with compassion on the whole human family; take away the arrogance and hatred which infect our hearts; break down the walls that separate us; unite us in bonds of love; and work through our struggle and confusion to accomplish your purposes on earth; that, in your good time, all nations and races may serve you in harmony around your heavenly throne; through Jesus Christ our Lord. Amen.

FOR PEACE

Eternal God, in whose perfect kingdom no sword is drawn but the sword of righteousness, no strength known but the strength of love: So mightily spread abroad your Spirit, that all peoples may be gathered under the banner of the Prince of Peace, as children of one Father; to whom be dominion and glory, now and for ever. Amen.

FOR PEACE AMONG THE NATIONS

Almighty God our heavenly Father, guide the nations of the world into the way of justice and truth, and establish among them that peace which is the fruit of righteousness, that they may become the kingdom of our Lord and Savior Jesus Christ. Amen.

FOR THE CHURCH

Gracious Father, we pray for thy holy catholic church. Fill it with all truth, in all truth with all peace. Where it is corrupt, purify it; where it is in error, direct it; where in any thing it is amiss, reform it. Where it is right, strengthen it; where it is in want, provide for it; where it is divided, reunite it; for the sake of Jesus Christ thy Son our Savior. Amen.

FOR THE PRESIDENT OF THE UNITED STATES AND ALL IN CIVIL AUTHORITY

O Lord our Governor, whose glory is in all the world: We commend this nation to thy merciful care, that, being guided by thy Providence, we may dwell secure in thy peace. Grant to the President of the United States, the Governor of this State, and to all in authority, wisdom and strength to know and to do thy will. Fill them with the love of truth and righteousness, and make them ever mindful of their calling to serve this people in thy fear; through Jesus Christ our Lord, who liveth and reigneth with thee and the Holy Spirit, one God, world without end. Amen.

FOR THOSE IN THE ARMED FORCES OF OUR COUNTRY

Almighty God, we commend to your gracious care and keeping all the men and women of our armed forces at home and abroad. Defend them day by day with your heavenly grace; strengthen them in their trials and temptations; give them courage to face the perils which beset them; and grant them a sense of your abiding presence wherever they may be; through Jesus Christ our Lord. Amen.

FOR FAMILIES

Almighty God, our heavenly Father, who settest the solitary in families: We commend to thy continual care the homes in which thy people dwell. Put far from them, we beseech thee, every root of bitterness, the desire of vainglory, and the pride of life. Fill them with faith, virtue, knowledge, temperance, patience, godliness. Knit together in constant affection those who, in holy wedlock, have been made one flesh. Turn the hearts of the parents to the children, and the hearts of the children to the parents; and so enkindle fervent charity among us all, that we may evermore be kindly affectioned one to another; through Jesus Christ our Lord. Amen.

FOR THE CARE OF CHILDREN

Almighty God, heavenly Father, you have blessed us with the joy and care of children: Give us calm strength and patient wisdom as we bring them up, that we may teach them to love whatever is just and true and good, following the example of our Savior Jesus Christ. Amen.

FOR A PERSON IN TROUBLE OR BEREAVEMENT

O merciful Father, who hast taught us in thy holy Word that thou dost not willingly afflict or grieve the children of men: Look with pity upon the sorrows of thy servant for whom our prayers are offered. Remember *him*, O Lord, in mercy, nourish *his* soul with patience, comfort *him* with a sense of thy goodness, lift up thy countenance upon *him*, and give *him* peace; through Jesus Christ our Lord. Amen.

FOR GUIDANCE

O God, by whom the meek are guided in judgment, and light riseth up in darkness for the godly: Grant us, in all our doubts and uncertainties, the grace to ask what thou wouldest have us to do, that the Spirit of wisdom may save us from all false choices, and that in thy light we may see light, and in thy straight path may not stumble; through Jesus Christ our Lord. Amen.

A GENERAL THANKSGIVING

Accept, O Lord, our thanks and praise for all that you have done for us. We thank you for the splendor of the whole creation, for the beauty of this world, for the wonder of life, and for the mystery of love. We thank you for the blessing of family and friends, and for the loving care which surrounds us on every side. We thank you for setting us at tasks which demand our best efforts, and for leading us to accomplishments which satisfy and delight us. We thank you also for those disappointments and failures that lead us to acknowledge our dependence on you alone. Above all, we thank you for your Son Jesus Christ; for the truth of his Word and the example of his life; for his steadfast obedience, by which he overcame temptation; for his dying, through which he overcame death; and for his rising to life again, in which we are raised to the life of your kingdom. Grant us the gift of your Spirit, that we may know him and make him known; and through him, at all times and in all places, may give thanks to you in all things. Amen.

FOR THE GIFT OF A CHILD

Heavenly Father, you sent your own Son into this world. We thank you for the life of this child, _____, entrusted to our care. Help us to remember that we are all your children, and so to love and nurture *him*, that *he* may attain to that full stature

253

intended for *him* in your eternal kingdom; for the sake of your dear Son, Jesus Christ our Lord. Amen.

NOTES

* Opening prayers are adapted from ancient hymn texts that are chanted at the Community of Jesus during the Divine Office. These texts are ascribed to various writers of the first millennium including Prudentius, Ambrose, Gregory, and Alcuin. The rhythms of the natural world, especially the cycle of day and night, are recurrent themes that are frequently used to reflect the character of their Creator.

The readings used for Morning Prayer have been taken from the following sources:

4   Thomas à Kempis, *The Imitation of Christ*, ed. Hal M. Helms (Brewster, MA: Paraclete Press, Inc., 1982), 117.

14 Hal M. Helms, *Echoes of Eternity*, Vol. 2 (Brewster, MA: Paraclete Press, Inc., 1998), 38.

22 Robert Benson, *That We May Perfectly Love Thee* (Brewster, MA: Paraclete Press, Inc., 2002), 63.

30 Frederica Mathewes-Green, *The Illumined Heart: The Ancient Christian Path of Transformation* (Brewster, MA: Paraclete Press, Inc., 2001), 41.

38 *The Confessions of Saint Augustine,* ed. Hal M. Helms (Brewster, MA: Paraclete Press, Inc., 1986), 1.

46 Linette Martin, *Sacred Doorways: A Beginner's Guide to Icons* (Brewster, MA: Paraclete Press, Inc., 2002), 218.

54 Daniel Homan, O.S.B., and Lonni Collins Pratt, *Radical Hospitality, Benedict's Way of Love* (Brewster, MA: Paraclete Press, Inc., 2002), 51.

64 François Fénelon, *Talking with God,* ed. Hal M. Helms (Brewster, MA: Paraclete Press, Inc., 1997), 56.

74 Cardinal Basil Hume, *The Mystery of the Incarnation* (Brewster, MA: Paraclete Press, Inc., 2000), 130.

82 à Kempis, *The Imitation of Christ,* 5.

90 Helms, *Echoes of Eternity,* 2.

98 *Talks on the Song of Songs, Bernard of Clairvaux,* ed. Bernard Bangley (Brewster, MA: Paraclete Press, Inc., 2002), 33.

106 W. Paul Jones, *Teaching the Dead Bird to Sing* (Brewster, MA: Paraclete Press, Inc., 2002), 36.

114 Jeremy Taylor, *Holy Living,* ed. Hal M. Helms (Brewster, MA: Paraclete Press, Inc., 1988), 40.

124 Brother Lawrence, *The Practice of the Presence of God,* trans. Robert J. Edmonson (Brewster, MA: Paraclete Press, Inc., 1985), 76.

134 Homan and Pratt, *Radical Hospitality,* xxxvii.

142 Jean-Pierre de Caussade, *The Joy of Full Surrender,* ed. Hal M. Helms (Brewster, MA: Paraclete Press, Inc., 1996), 152.

150 Robert Waldron, *Blue Hope* (Brewster, MA: Paraclete Press, Inc., 2002), 71.

158 Teresa of Avila, *The Way of Perfection,* ed. Henry L. Carrigan, Jr. (Brewster, MA: Paraclete Press, Inc., 2000), 101.

166 M. Basil Pennington, O.C.S.O., *Seeking His Mind, 40 Meetings with Christ* (Brewster, MA: Paraclete Press, Inc., 2002), 84.

174 Taylor, *Holy Living,* 22.

184 Margaret Silf, *Sacred Spaces, Stations on a Celtic Way* (Brewster, MA: Paraclete Press, Inc., 2001), 54.

193 *Eternal Wisdom from the Desert,* ed. Henry L. Carrigan, Jr. (Brewster, MA: Paraclete Press, Inc., 2001), 78.

201 John of the Cross, *Ascent of Mount Carmel,* ed. Henry L. Carrigan, Jr. (Brewster, MA: Paraclete Press, Inc., 2002), 23.

209 Cindy Crosby, *By Willoway Brook: Exploring the Landscape of Prayer* (Brewster, MA: Paraclete Press, Inc., 2003), 130.

217 Pennington, *Seeking His Mind,* 98.

225 *The Temple, The Poetry of George Herbert,* ed. Henry L. Carrigan, Jr. (Brewster, MA: Paraclete Press, Inc., 2001), 21.

233 Fénelon, *Talking with God,* 18.

ABOUT PARACLETE PRESS

Who We Are

Paraclete Press is an ecumenical publisher of books and recordings on Christian spirituality. Our publishing represents a full expression of Christian belief and practice—from Catholic to Evangelical, from Protestant to Orthodox.

Paraclete Press is the publishing arm of the Community of Jesus, an ecumenical monastic community in the Benedictine tradition. As such, we are uniquely positioned in the marketplace without connection to a large corporation and with informal relationships to many branches and denominations of faith.

We like it best when people buy our books from booksellers, our partners in successfully reaching as wide an audience as possible.

What We Are Doing

Books

Paraclete Press publishes books that show the richness and depth of what it means to be Christian. Although Benedictine spirituality is at the heart of all that we do, we publish books that reflect the Christian experience across many cultures, time periods, and houses of worship.

We publish books that nourish the vibrant life of the church and its people—books about spiritual practice, formation, history, ideas, and customs.

We have several different series of books within Paraclete Press, including the best-selling Living Library series of modernized classic texts; A Voice from the Monastery—giving voice to men and women monastics about what it means to live a spiritual life today; award-winning literary faith fiction; and books that explore Judaism and Islam and discover how these faiths inform Christian thought and practice.

Recordings

From Gregorian chant to contemporary American choral works, our music recordings celebrate the richness of sacred choral music through the centuries. Paraclete is proud to distribute the recordings of the internationally acclaimed choir Gloriæ Dei Cantores, who have been praised for their "rapt and fathomless spiritual intensity" by *American Record Guide,* and the Gloriæ Dei Cantores Schola, which specializes in the study and performance of Gregorian chant. Paraclete is also the exclusive North American distributor of the recordings of the Monastic Choir of St. Peter's Abbey in Solesmes, France, long considered to be a leading authority on Gregorian chant performance.

Learn more about us at our Web site:
www.paracletepress.com,
or call us toll-free at
1-800-451-5006.